RENEGADE
OF LIGHT

Preface by Dennis E. Higgins

There I sat, in my car, motionless and in deep contemplation. I once had a lucrative job, assets, real estate, investments and a 401k that guaranteed me an early retirement. And then, in 2005, our own government gave the corporations the green light to screw the working class here at home by sending our manufacturing jobs to China and India. Then, in 2008, when the bankers got together with their criminal friends on Wall Street and intentionally crashed the market, I learned that everything was rigged against us and there were no guarantees in life at all except death and taxes. Everything I believed in; everything I had worked so hard to obtain throughout the years, was suddenly stripped away, including my beloved Great Dane friend whom I was no longer able to care for. The pain culminated when our eyes locked through the rear-view window of his new owner's car as it drove away. Rest well, old friend. It was in this stunned state that I wondered how something so good could have gone so bad. While re-evaluating my life, I received my first potent message from my very soul that contacted me when my world was broken and shattered, "Now that I have your attention, we can do what we came here to do." When our lives need a new direction, the soul will find a way to reach out to the human self to bring about its destiny. I understood then, that an eternal, immortal soul has no need of money or assets or investments and it certainly has no intention of ever retiring. I found that losing everything is when the real journey of self-discovery begins.

Little did I know that the brilliant work of Barbara Marciniak's 'Bringers of the Dawn,' the combined research of David Icke, Gary Zukov, George Kavassilas, and many others would one day collectively contribute to this adventure I was embroiled in. Though I always knew something was wrong with the world the way it is, their passionate work encouraged me to reveal what they found in the darkest depths of the rabbit hole. I began to discern the lies, the deception, and the manipulation which had been intentionally woven throughout all aspects of society that have plagued humanity throughout the ages. I learned, through their research and personal experience that the true nature of humanity had been cleverly hidden by those who seek to control and oppress it. This deep, esoteric knowledge, revealed by these very brave researchers could shock the world to its core if it could ever become known to the general public on a massive scale. I knew, as I have always known, that it was my purpose on earth to present astounding information to the world at large when the time was right, and thus, 'Renegade of Light' was born.

The revelations in the story are every bit as exciting and awe-inspiring as the times we are living in today. People across the globe know that something is wrong with the world. People are ready and mature enough now to hear this message about our true heritage and the forces that have hijacked our perception. As uncomfortable as the truth is, when the time is right, the truth will ultimately set us free.

This novel is intended to help humanity break free from the confines of the fear-based reality we collectively find ourselves in and return once again to a love-based reality, in harmony and oneness with our galactic family and our Universal Creator.

Preface by Jason McLeod

I have spent a great deal of my life delving into the deepest secrets of the world. It began in my early teens, when I realized that I was immersed in and was a part of a flawless, intelligent design of an unimaginable size, scope and scale. I understood that I was an intricate part of the collective whole. I knew, therefore, that Creator was an all-encompassing field of awareness and I could never be apart from it. It was this inner knowing that afforded me a feeling of peace and a sense of great comfort.

I have always known that I had chosen to incarnate on earth to participate in something far greater than myself. I knew I would serve my fellow man and all life on this beautiful planet by fulfilling a very special role, not because I was any more special than anyone else, but because I chose to devote my life to help others understand who they were, why they came here and what they would experience when the bodies they were using ceased to function.

As synchronicity would have it, when I was ready, the Universal Creator brought me together with the late Ed and Lorraine Warren, two of the most astounding people I have ever known, people whom I would come to call teachers, mentors and friends. The Warrens took me under their wings and enabled me to explore the unseen world of spirit phenomena and it was under their guidance and counsel that I had my first incredible psychic experiences which enabled me to begin to understand the nature of the reality I found myself in.

When I came upon my first Metaphysical bookstore, I discovered more missing pieces to the puzzle I had been putting together through the years.

One will never find deep, esoteric knowledge in mainstream publications, not because the information isn't real, but because its spread would threaten the System which has been in place for millennia for the purpose of hiding the truth from the masses.

The information you are about to read is not fantasy or science fiction.

It is fact.

RENEGADE OF LIGHT

by

Jason McLeod

**Created from the Original Screenplay
by Dennis E. Higgins**

RENEGADE OF LIGHT

First Edition © 2019 by Jason Montgomery McLeod and
Dennis E. Higgins
ALL RIGHTS RESERVED

Cover art by: Todd Hebertson
Editor: Tom Kimball, Ph.D.

Print layout and eBook editions by booknook.biz

This edition first printing: August 2019

ISBN: 9781097452439
ISBN (ebook) 978-0-9884451-9-2

Please visit our website:
www.renegadeoflight.com

Please visit the author's websites:
www.mcleodmetaphysics.com & www.darksiege.com

Dedication

This book is dedicated to the Wayshowers, the Starseeds, the Luminaries, and all beings who, from far away, came to Earth in service to Earth, Humanity and Creator, to help facilitate the greatest mass-expansion in consciousness this world has ever known.

Notable authors, channels, directors, experiencers, investigators, producers, radio hosts, researchers, scientists, and speakers on the forefront are by no means limited to:

Mike Bara
Bashar
Art Bell
Santos Bonacci
Dolores Cannon
Barbara Hand Clow
Colonel Phillip Corso
Erich von Daniken
Laura Eisenhower
Stanton Friedman
Foster Gamble
James Gilliland
Corey Goode
Dr. Steven Greer
Graham Hancock
Nassim Haramein
Paul Hellyer
William Henry

Linda Moulton Howe

David Icke

George Kavassilas

Kryon

Glen A. Larson

Bob Lazar

James Mahu and the Wingmakers

Barbara Marciniak

Jim Marrs

Jordan Maxwell

Billy Meir

George Noory

Jimmy Roberts

Patricia Cota-Robles

Gene Roddenberry

Dr. Michael Salla

Robert M. Schoch

Zecharia Sitchin

Emery Smith

Robert Steele

Whitley Strieber

Michael Tellinger

Admiral Bill Thomkins

George Tsoukalos

Neale Donald Walsch

David Wilcock

Gary Zukav

Special Thanks

This book was in part made possible through a contribution made by:

Jonathan Rick

This collaboration would not have come together without the coordination made possible by Jean Kruse-Blasingame and the generous support of our editor Tom Kimball, Ph.D., our outstanding artist, Todd Hebertson and our website designer Brian Fiske. We would also like to recognize the dedication and professionalism of the many fine people at booknook.biz, especially Kimberly Hitchens and Barb. Thank you for all that you do.

The authors would like to recognize the many wonderful, enlightened beings of the two Austin Texas-based Circle of Intention Meetings for tireless service and dedication in the ongoing collective effort to awaken humanity and affect great change through meditative intention.

We highly recommend reading the following books which were the foundation of the Circle of Intention Meetings which have been gathering twice a week for over a decade:

The Handbook for the New Paradigm
Embracing the Rainbow
Becoming
Messages for the Ground Crew

About the Screenwriter

Dennis E. Higgins has devoted several years of his life earnestly studying the plethora of groundbreaking information revealed by some of the most respected and accomplished researchers in the fields of extraterrestrial civilizations and their involvement with the human species on earth. The information gleaned from these astounding men and women inspired Higgins to write the screenplay for an intriguing feature film, specifically and most importantly, the amazing material published in Barbara Marciniak's

BRINGERS OF THE DAWN
Teachings from the Pleiadians

About the Author

Jason McLeod is an intuitive empath, spiritualist and paranormal investigator who has spent the majority of his life delving into the hidden and mysterious secrets of the world under the careful guidance of none other than the legendary **Ed and Lorraine Warren**—the late pioneers of the modern ghost hunting craze that thrives to this day.

The incredible phenomena McLeod had personally witnessed and experienced beginning with the very first case he had investigated on the Warrens' behalf in 1990 and on the many intriguing cases he had investigated alongside them that followed, allowed McLeod to begin to understand the true nature of the multidimensional reality that humanity and all life is an integral part of.

While working with the Warrens and while attending Sacred Heart University, McLeod wrote the newspaper column 'Hauntings,' which revealed the information he was learning from the Warrens and the intricate details about the cases that were currently under investigation at that time.

After transferring to Washington State to finish his Creative Writing Degree, Lorraine Warren called McLeod and asked him to investigate a case in nearby Rathdrum, Idaho as the lead investigator on their behalf. The bizarre case was yet another synchronicity which enabled McLeod to meet Valerie Crisp, Barbara Doede and the late Bruce Tainio, an incredible group of psychics, visionaries and scientists—powerful lightworkers who became instant life-long friends, mentors and colleagues, people who enabled McLeod to expand his awareness and consciousness even further, to prepare him for the profound sojourn they were all undertaking together for the purpose of benefiting humanity.

McLeod started writing his '*Hauntings*' column for the Eastern Washington University Easterner Newspaper and formed the Northwest Society for Paranormal Research there in 1992, where he and his new colleagues revealed their vast collective knowledge to intrigued college students and to the general population at large in the Greater Spokane Area.

Soon after, McLeod was inundated with personal letters received from people who were experiencing unexplained paranormal phenomena themselves, including, most remarkably, cases involving intelligent beings of an extraterrestrial nature. After investigating several of those cases personally, McLeod experienced a benevolent, awe-inspiring connection with a group of those same extraterrestrials himself, an event which changed the course and focus of his life completely.

Following his graduation, McLeod returned home to Connecticut and it is there that he became embroiled in the most fascinating and frightening paranormal case he had ever experienced to date. It was a case he self-published in his bestselling debut novel, *Dark Siege: A Connecticut Family's Nightmare*, the Kindle version of which held the #1 bestsellers rank in all three listing categories on Amazon for several weeks at a time, on multiple occasions and the top ten rank for many months.

Because there was more to tell, McLeod sent a second completed manuscript to his friend and colleague Bishop James Long, the presiding Archbishop of the United States Old Catholic Church. He expressed his reservations about releasing the much-anticipated sequel because of the intense graphic nature of the diabolical attacks unleashed upon the family just two months after the case had been successfully resolved. After reading the manuscript, which he read in one day, Long not only encouraged McLeod to release it, without withholding any of the disturbing details of the attacks, but he also promised to make both books required reading for his Demonology Class, so that his students could understand the very serious dangers involved with dabbling in the negative occult. McLeod immediately self-published the spine-tingling sequel, *Dark Siege: The Nightmare Returns*. After Long discussed the *Dark Siege Series* on *Coast to Coast AM* in 2015, McLeod was invited on the same program with co-host Connie Willis on April 12, 2015.

Today, McLeod conducts engaging presentations on radio blog broadcasts, at paranormal conventions, spirituality expositions, New Age events, libraries and lecture halls throughout the world, where he reveals his profound understanding that all things everywhere are part of a flawless, perfect, intelligent design. This has enabled him to bridge the gap between science and spirituality, to easily explain the paranormal through Quantum Physics, the Universal Laws of Attraction, Intention and Manifestation.

McLeod's first-hand experiences have led him to conclude that all life forms in the Multiverse, both seen and unseen, are individuated aspects of the totality of Source / Creator, and that all life is sacred.

He believes that the underlying purpose of the synchronistic events in his life, which unfolded precisely at the right times, were meant for him to assist humanity by helping them remember their true Divine Nature.

The subject of Ascension has always fascinated him, due to a deeply-rooted knowing that all expressing consciousness seeks to grow; to expand and ultimately evolve into higher states of awareness. It was also explained to him, by the extraterrestrials, that he would prove integral in the planetary transformation when the time came and that nothing could stop his own personal Ascension.

McLeod's most recent release, *Our Journey Home: The Handbook for the Transition* is a beautiful and inspiring large-print, illustrated paperback through which one can truly understand the natural process of withdrawing their awareness from their physical bodies when they are no longer capable of supporting their consciousness and what they will experience before, during, and afterwards.

McLeod, like his many mentors, friends and colleagues, have devoted their lives to the study and thorough understanding of the serious risks, rewards and ramifications of investigating the unseen world of the paranormal. It takes someone of great faith, strength, power, and determination to stand boldly against the malevolent forces seeking the ruination of mankind. McLeod can think of no better teachers and mentors than Ed and Lorraine Warren, who have risked their lives many times over to root out, expose, challenge, and expel the forces of diabolical evil; of powers and principalities and a hierarchy seeking to control and dominate all life in this world. He is grateful for that rare privilege and maintains contact with many of his colleagues to this day.

When McLeod read Dennis E. Higgins' screenplay, *Renegade of Light*, he knew he had the perfect opportunity to use his accumulated esoteric knowledge and cinematic writing style to expand upon the information Dennis had presented in his original screenplay and write the perfect novel adaptation of the riveting information that the story delves into.

Introduction

The eternal, all-knowing, all-encompassing Source of all Creation made available for each of the infinitesimal souls it had created, through the most selfless act of pure unconditional love, the option to voluntarily and temporarily leave the highest spiritual dimensions.

These individuated fields of conscious awareness, these immortal, eternal, unconquerable offspring were then cast into the limitless realms of creation for the sole purpose, the soul-purpose of knowing themselves as unique aspects of the totality of the whole.

As they voluntarily departed from the highest spiritual dimensions, they were gently encouraged to evolve into the greatest versions of the grandest visions of whomever they chose to become, for such sojourns were intended *always* for the highest good of themselves; for one another; for their Creator and for all of Creation.

To ensure their safety, legions of angels and learned souls who had themselves returned to Source from their own paths of self-discovery, were dispatched to guide, watch over, encourage and protect them.

A fail safe was set in place from the very beginning of this great experiment, for Creator knew some volunteers would go astray, and at great risk to themselves and to the many others who would willfully follow them or be negatively affected by them, amnesia would overcome them and they would forget Who They Are, where they came from, and what their original purpose was.

This plan, known throughout Creation as 'The Great Awakening,' would activate at specific intervals, known only to Creator Itself, should those souls who had embarked upon the journey fail to remember and become hopelessly lost without the slightest hope of returning 'Home' without such loving and divine assistance.

This Event would involve the sudden, glorious explosion of pure unconditional love from Creator's heart. This clarion call would reverberate throughout and encompass all layers and dimensions throughout Creation. It would traverse the great expanse of the multiverse, cascading throughout the universe and every galaxy within. It would cause each Sun, one after the other, to emit a Solar Flash one-thousand-times brighter than the Suns themselves, until every planet orbiting around them was affected.

This unstoppable wave of pure Light would penetrate and permeate everything it came into contact with, for nothing could thwart Creator's plan. It would, no matter how far they have strayed or how low they have fallen, restore all sentient beings to their fully-activated, fully-empowered divine template.

This Ascension Wave would then revitalize, rejuvenate, restore, and reconnect all sentient beings with the light, love, and heart-centered compassion of the Creator. It would ensure that every individuation could, if they so choose, return 'Home' once again to the highest spiritual dimensions from which they originated and arrive there completely and utterly unscathed with all of the knowledge and wisdom they had accumulated throughout their travels into and out of form.

Chapter 1

THE GREAT, SCINTILLATING SPIRAL ARMS of the Milky Way galaxy churned slowly in the vast, cold reaches of space. Each brilliant speck of light within was itself one of an incalculable number of life-sustaining Stars which fed and nourished the innumerable worlds orbiting around them, which in turn, were host to a bountiful variety of sentient life forms.

Brightness knew no equal when the massive explosion of Divine Light energy erupted out of the great central Sun at the core of the galaxy, radiating unhindered and reaching out toward Earth and to its inhabitants who were about to be completely and forever changed.

Many hundreds of thousands of years in the distant past, 23 races of advanced, enlightened beings came together to participate in the greatest genetic experiment the galaxy had ever known. Operating from the orbit around Earth in a massive, spherical, space station laboratory, each race eagerly contributed to the effort to create a glorious new race of Galactic Beings. Because all participating races declared their intention was for the highest and best good of all, The Universal Creator agreed to endow each human with a higher consciousness and thus the magnificent Human Race was born—a race of fully-connected beings with twelve strands of DNA whose genetic coding provided them with the best attributes that each unique species had to offer.

The great experiment ushered in an era of peace and tranquility where fully-connected Humans walked the Earth as gods, enjoying blissful oneness and harmony with all life forms on the planet and with The Universal Creator—a dance in perfect union with the infinite conscious awareness inherent in all things.

With Creator's blessing, the genetically-engineered race of humans would be given the freedom to grow and evolve under the careful guidance and protection of its many Progenitor races, so when the time was right, humanity could rise to take its place as a permanent part of the galactic family.

However, once they had learned of this experiment and the newly-created species, dark, ruthless Reptilian beings from the Draco Constellation invaded the Sol system with their immense and powerful battle fleet. In the brief, one-sided conflict which followed, the Draco fleet defeated the Pleiadians and devastated the orbital science station's meager defenses. The Reptilians boarded and converted it for their own use. To disguise its true nature, and the effects of their meddling from the many interstellar races which were likely to pass by, they amassed enough silica from nearby systems to cover the base's entire surface well enough to cause it to appear as a natural, organic satellite or moon.

The Draco then took possession of the Earth, a planet they found much to their liking, with a climate and ecosystem similar, if not identical to their home planets and the greatest prize of all—the orphaned new species left defenseless to fend for themselves without knowing who they were, why they were there, or what their intended future would have offered them if it had not been so suddenly stripped away.

The Draco quickly learned that the new experimental species was far too connected and conscious to subjugate as they had done to the many other beings they had conquered throughout the galaxy. They discovered that the enlightened humans, armed with their enhanced connection and creativity would be a threat too powerful to contain should they ever rise in sufficient numbers to oppose them. Though they knew it would make the planet much less hospitable for Reptilian kind, they cut the space station's power, which initiated the irreversible, instantaneous collapse of the persistent precipitation band it had been maintaining around the equator to create and maintain the paradise on Earth the Progenitors had intended for humanity.

The Draco were confident that the threat that the new species would pose to their dominion would be eliminated forever, save for the select few humans they elected to keep alive for their own nefarious purposes.

And so, The Great Deluge swept every trace of the new species and their existence from the surface of the Earth and buried it all beneath hundreds of feet of thick mud, silt and debris. All that once was would forever be shrouded in mystery and intrigue for generations to come.

The Draco, who were known across the galaxy as master geneticists themselves, soon initiated their own genetic alterations and experiments on the small number of survivors, to undo what the Progenitor races had accomplished collectively. Though they knew they could never fully separate humanity from Universal Creator, they began a systematic campaign to do everything in their power to diminish that connection as much as possible, as well as to cut off humanity from the dormant information locked permanently and securely away in their encoded twelve-helix DNA—innate knowledge and proof that humanity was never alone in the universe, but had instead, intimate cosmic connections to vast, galactic civilizations.

The Draco shunted and dumbed down this new Galactic Race by devolving humanity down to a limited, two-helix DNA system which rendered them barely conscious, and continually focused on their own survival, so that they would never be capable of mounting any kind of organized resistance.

It was not enough for them to dominate and control humanity. The Draco had to make their slaves more like themselves. So, through time, they genetically-engineered the implementation of the Reptilian brain and with it, their instincts of self-preservation, territoriality, aggression, aggressive reproduction, ego, and associated negative emotions—fear, anger, greed, jealousy, anxiety, and a fight or flight mentality to further keep their slaves fragmented, divided, and unable to trust even one another.

Furthermore, to blind humanity's psychic sight, they dimmed the higher frequency connection the Progenitors made possible through enhancing what they knew to be the Seat of the Soul—the pine cone-shaped, photosensitive pineal gland sitting directly in the center of both the left and right hemispheres of the human brain.

To further disconnect their new slave race, the Draco immediately began conducting negative rituals at the epicenters of the major energy vortices to shunt Earth's energy field, which they knew would further suppress humanity, *vibrationally*, by forcing the entire planet and everything on it into an extra low-frequency environment.

To ensure that humanity was firmly and permanently within their stranglehold, they created systems of control which ensured that division, tribal mentality, interpersonal conflicts, and wars would keep the population in a constant state of frustration and one full of fear, anger, despair, and hopelessness.

They maintained their iron grip through the millennia from the space station by relaying an artificial, holographic fear-based control grid matrix from signals sent directly from the rings of Saturn—a Draco owned frequency broadcasting system of gargantuan proportions.

Finally, the Reptilians knew there would be no greater method of control than by ensuring that humanity would be completely oblivious about their dominion over them. So, they greatly reduced humanity's ability to perceive things as they truly were, by limiting their ability to see only but the tiniest fraction of the electromagnetic spectrum known as visible light, which was less than 1% of the matter, space, and energy surrounding them.

This ancient, malevolent inter-dimensional race of Reptilians, operating just beyond the range of limited human perception, had therefore locked humanity into a false holographic matrix of fear, chaos, and control, from which, they knew, few in their entire lifetimes would ever escape, without outside help from forces operating from a state of expanded awareness.

They also knew that time was short, for they had violated Universal Law and help was on the way...

Chapter 2

THE THICK, EARLY MORNING HAZE sat heavily over the pre-dawn downtown streets of Austin, Texas. Pools of rain-water had collected during the night, reflecting the soft over-head glow of the many streetlights—stalwart sentinels which lent a sense of order and security to an otherwise chaotic and crime-ridden part of town.

The dilapidated, rusted brown Chevy Cavalier sedan groaned as it turned widely from an alley onto East 12th Street. Its balding tires sloshed through the many oil-ridden puddles and squealed as they fought to regain their grip on the steaming blacktop when the car slowly accelerated. The driver's side front window slipped down inside the door and out came both a disheveled Caucasian man's bruised elbow which he promptly rested on the top edge of the door and the low, discordant resonant sound of unrelenting death metal music. The driver reflexively glanced into the cracked side-view mirror and when he saw nothing to be concerned about, he cracked a smile, exposing his crooked, yellow, nicotine-stained teeth and leaned his head back onto the torn leatherette head rest. He held the grimy steering wheel loosely between his left thumb and forefinger, checked both the rear-view mirror and the speedometer and then turned to regard the passenger.

The passenger, an emaciated, greasy-haired, 23-year-old Guatemalan, rapped his fingers on the dashboard. As the beats on the stereo intensified, he coiled his filthy hands into fists and pounded them against the glove box and moved them in succession across and down the center console. Smiling deviously, he peeled his jaundiced, yellowed eyes away from the center console and up toward his most recent accomplice.

"Yeah!" the driver cheered. "Oh, hell yeah, dude!"

The passenger smiled knowingly.

"That's what I'm talkin' about," the driver said with a broad smile. "Those punks bought that blow up like they were kids in a candy store. We're really on to something, man! This powder is cash!"

The passenger pursed his lips and nodded. "That was way too easy, bruh!"

The driver grinned. "That deal was the easiest we've ever scored." He turned his attention away for a split second to make sure the coast was clear on the road ahead of them. "It put us over five-grand, I'd say." When he looked back and focused on his accomplice, his eyes grew wider and wider.

The passenger was dangling a tiny plastic Ziploc bag containing finely-ground cocaine powder inside. He jostled it before his friend and grinned. "Leftovers for us!"

"God damn!" he boomed. "This is the life."

They bumped fists and proceeded to bang their heads to the music as it thumped through the speakers.

As they crept along, less than a mile ahead of them, the first rays of pulsating golden-white light from the Galactic Central Sun had finally reached the Earth, pierced the heavens and streaked down from the early morning sky. It struck the jet-black Dodge Charger police interceptor parked on the side of the road concealed in-between the Spectrum Cable TV truck and the orange construction signs where Detective Danny Phelps sat inside, listening patiently to the police scanner for the first signs of trouble. The high-vibrational ray passed effortlessly through the red and blue emergency light bar and white-painted roof, moved through the thin, black interior liner and shot directly into the center of the top of Danny Phelps' head. Completely unaware that anything out of the ordinary had happened, the seasoned veteran police detective's entire scalp and thick black hair erupted into a perpetual, flickering violet flame.

Phelps cocked his ear and shifted his eyes to the mirrors when he caught the faintest hints of the approaching music. He knew, instinctively, that only troublemakers were up so early on a Saturday morning, selfishly blasting their music through a sleeping residential neighborhood. Suddenly, a scintillating indigo-colored light swirled around the inner-most hairs of his eyebrows and erupted from the center of his forehead. Although he felt a slight tingle in the region, he saw absolutely nothing in the mirror—even though his eyes were fixed directly inside it.

Outside and beyond the range of his limited human per-ception, a chain reaction was now cascading from the entry point in the crown of his head, down between his eyes, and descending to affect his entire body.

Phelps ran his pointer finger between the collar of his shirt and his cleanly-shaven neck at an uncomfortable tickle growing there. He then felt a sudden urgency in his chest. He thrust a clenched fist to his mouth and coughed just as an indiscernible blue light flashed out of the front of his neck and hovered there near his throat.

Then, a bright green flame danced counterclockwise around his heart and moved effortlessly around his chest until a pulsating geometric pattern floated before his dark blue shirt.

He drew an uncommonly deep breath and when he exhaled, a bright yellow light emanated from his solar plexus region and sat there, flickering and shimmering like a minia-ture version of the Sun.

The process continued as an orange light expanded out of his sacrum and set his entire pelvis aglow. It saturated his Glock 23mm sidearm and twinkled while loitering there.

Finally, a glowing red sphere passed out of his body from his tail bone and flashed continually below his seat.

The individual colored lights hanging in a perfect ver-tical line just six inches from the front of his body, spun in unison until the interior of the entire car erupted in a blinding white flash. Phelps merely blinked his eyes in response. Little did he know that something extraordinary had just occurred—something that would change his life and the future of humanity forever.

The music grew louder and that's when Phelps spot-ted the weathered sedan in his side-view mirror. He firmly gripped the shifter and grinned at the prospect of reeling in his first catch of the day.

As the amateur drug dealers drew closer, the driver snatched the bag of coke from his partner in crime and kissed it tenderly. He squeezed the bag gently but firmly in his palm and closed his eyes briefly as if it were a gift handed down to them by the gods. He smiled and handed it back to his buddy who began to peel open the tiny seam with his fingers.

The passenger nodded and was just about to drive his finger into the bag when he noticed the look of horror on the driver's face as he stared into the rear-view mirror and turned the music off.

"What's up?" pleaded the passenger.

The adrenaline was already coursing through the driv-er's body as he ran his hand down over his face to wake himself up. "I think that's a cop behind us!"

The passenger whipped his head around reflexively.

The driver scowled, "Shit, man, don't turn around!"

Realizing his mistake, the passenger began to panic himself. He pointed rapidly at the upcoming stop sign. "Turn the fucking corner!"

The brakes squealed as they came to a complete stop at the intersection. The three seconds they waited felt like an eternity until the driver cut the wheel and hit the gas.

"Did he pass yet?" the passenger whelped.

Gritting his teeth, the driver said, "No, God damn it!" His knuckles turned white as he tightened his grip on the wheel, scanning the roadway for any avenue of escape. He turned his head toward the passenger. "Stash that blow!"

Bewildered, the passenger looked around frantically. Finally, he pleaded, "Where, man?"

The driver roared, "Just stash it, man! Anywhere out of sight!"

Phelps retained his sharp focus on the car ahead of him, waiting for the license plate information the scanner mounted in the front of his cruiser obtained to return from headquarters and appear on his on-board laptop screen. As he waited, he drew a deep breath and moved his hair back with a quick flip of his wrist and was oblivious that the Light that had been interacting with him had faded away without a trace. He maintained his distance until the information he had been waiting for finally materialized. The car was properly registered *and insured*. He knew then that there was no legal justification to pull them over.

Phelps narrowed his eyes momentarily, weighing his options. He then smiled and pressed his foot down on the accelerator. Phelps closed the distance enough for him to clearly see the driver's eyes, now drawn wide with terror in the piece of junk's rear-view mirror when he anticipated the glow of the flashing red and blue emergency lights—the heralds of their approaching doom.

"Shit, dude!" shouted the driver. "He's gonna pull us over!"

Phelps narrowed his eyes, and with a forced southern drawl, he said, "Okay, ya'll..."

He flicked the necessary switch and the red and blue flashing lights erupted a millisecond later. "Let's have some fun!"

"Son of a bitch!"

The passenger tried vainly to ease his panic. "Be cool! Chill, man! He ain't got shit on us!"

The driver turned into a sleazy neighborhood and finally pulled over to the side of the curb and turned off the engine. The menacing police interceptor pulled in directly behind them and came to a stop. Much to their surprise, the cop had turned the emergency lights off, but the duo would soon discover that this was simply meant to avoid attracting unwanted attention.

Phelps was out of his cruiser quickly. He held his left hand over the handheld radio transmitter attached securely to his chest and positioned his right hand over his sidearm holster for a full 30 seconds, enough time, he knew, to completely terrorize the occupants of the car.

After a few moments, Phelps strolled over to the driver's side door, peered inside and rapped on the window with the first two fingers of his right hand.

The driver studied him nervously and rolled down his window. "Good morning, Officer. Is there a problem, sir?"

Phelps chuckled. He was actually impressed that the dirtbag could concoct a perfectly constructed sentence and deliver his inquiry in such a polite manner. Rather than answer him though, Phelps made a point to make it obvious that he was studying the interior of the vehicle to frighten them further. He scanned the center console area for a few more moments and then issued a command. "License and proof of financial responsibility!" He saw the look of obvious discomfort on the driver's face. He moved his right hand over to his holster again and leaned in closer, locking eyes with the passenger whose jaw hung slack.

Phelps' eyes carefully followed the driver's hands as he reached over and pulled the lever on the glovebox. The passenger did, too, and he was visibly tense and quiet. The passenger recoiled when the glove box fell open and the contents shifted inside. To Phelps, the panicked look in the passenger's eyes spoke volumes.

While the driver retrieved the documents he'd been asked for, Phelps asked. "Is this motor vehicle registered in your name?"

"Yes, sir!" he replied, as he fumbled with his wallet. When he had retrieved his driver's license, he handed it respectfully and cautiously to the waiting detective.

Phelps snatched the license and other documents he had been handed, but he didn't even bother to look at them. Instead, he reached up to make sure the volume knob on his transmitter was off and looked around him to see if anyone was watching. The passenger sneered at him as Phelps thrust his pointer finger at them both. "You know why I pulled you over, right?"

"No, I don't!" The driver exclaimed. "I wasn't doing anything wrong!" he added confidently.

"Because I felt like it!"

The passenger guffawed and the driver puffed up his chest in defiance. He drew a deep breath. "Uh, excuse me, officer. Because you felt like it? I don't think so!" He leaned in closer to him and continued. "Ever hear of probable cause? It's in the Fourth Amendment. Don't they teach you that... in cop school?"

Phelps snickered. He leaned in and jeered the driver with a confused expression, "Fourth what? Probable cause? I told you why I pulled you over. Did you forget already? Sit there and shut the hell up while I check your sorry ass for warrants!"

As Phelps walked nonchalantly back toward his car, the passenger wheeled around and waited until the cop was out of earshot before he unloaded on his friend. "Are you out of your fuckin' mind, bruh?" He flung his hands before him to accentuate his disgust. "Talkin' smack to a cop when we're carrying blow?" This ain't no illegal lane change, this is serious shit!"

The driver maintained a lock on Phelps in the side-view mirror. He said to his friend, without even turning to face him, "Chill, man. That prick can't do a damned thing! He's messing with the wrong American. I told him he has no probable cause and he just ignored me. It's all on the record. He's probably just another brain-dead pig abusing the people he's supposed to be serving and protecting."

The passenger slouched in his seat, held his face in his hands and shook his head repeatedly.

Detective Phelps studied them intently from within his squad car. The report came back from dispatch that the driver had no outstanding warrants, as he had anticipated. Phelps leaned back in his seat and his face went suddenly blank as he drifted into an altered state of consciousness. He began reciting something—though nothing audible issued forth from his lips.

Before they could believe it, the cop was peering inside the driver's side window again. After a momentary pause, he locked eyes with the driver and said, "Get out of the vehicle." Before the passenger could even challenge the unlawful order, Phelps pointed a threatening finger at the passenger and continued, "You, too, son!"

Moments later, as the orange glow of the rising Sun was

beaming directly down upon them, both frightened young men were standing outside the car on the driver's side.

"Face the car, hands on the roof!" Phelps commanded. "Spread your legs!"

The cool and collected driver protested. "What's the problem, officer?"

Phelps proceeded to run his hands down the front and back sides of the driver and around his waist. Then, he jammed his hands up the insides of his legs into his groin, so he could start on his legs. The perp knew better than to resist and his nostrils flared as he simply endured it all and allowed the cop to abuse him further.

Phelps grinned as he approached the sickly-looking Hispanic who was returning his gaze with narrowed eyes awaiting his turn. "Where's your Green Card?"

"I ain't got no damned Green Card, man!"

"You legal?" Phelps pressured, turning the corner of his mouth down in a scowl.

"The only illegal shit going down here is what *you're* doin', man!"

After he had frisked both young men, he snorted, "Hands behind your backs!"

"What?" they shouted defiantly and in unison. "Are you serious?"

Phelps jammed the driver's forearm behind his back to cut him off and held it securely by the wrist. He screamed out in pain, but didn't resist like the cop was most likely hoping he would. He knew the guy was as dirty as they come. Phelps moved him over to the grass and forced him to sit there. When he turned to cuff the passenger, the driver shouted, "Ah, man! It's wet..."

Phelps wheeled around and pointed at him. "Shut up!"

The passenger shook his head from side to side and positioned his hands behind his back, so he could easily be cuffed. He too, knew this cop was capable of nearly anything shady.

Phelps stood behind him and studied him. He leaned over and sniffed his neck. After a brief pause, he said, "You know what?"

"What?" the passenger retorted, angrily.

"You... stink!"

He slapped the kid's wrists and said, "Higher!"

"Huh?"

"Move your arms higher up toward the center of your back!"

"You can't stand that I'm cooperating with you the way I am, huh? You need to abuse me further, cop?"

Phelps slapped the metal cuff around the kid's wrist with enough force to cause him to wince. Phelps soaked it all in. He enjoyed punishing dirtbags whom he knew were up to no good, even when he couldn't actually prove anything. He knew there were always opportunities to escalate things during stops like these. But not this time. He knew everything about these perps. He was there for one reason: to rob them. When he had him firmly bound, he shoved him over toward the grass to sit him down beside his friend.

He stood there for a full minute and studied them. The young men locked eyes with him and then lowered them. They repeated the process three times in all until Phelps placed his hands on his hips and wheeled his head toward the vehicle. "You fellas wouldn't mind if I searched er' would ya?" He spat toward their feet.

The driver scoffed. "Hell, yeah, I mind. I do not consent to any searches! You have a search warrant?"

Phelps grinned from ear to ear. "Okay thanks," he said, nodding.

The driver hopped up and down as the shady cop walked

briskly over to his car. "Hey, you got no right to search my car! You got no probable cause!"

Phelps ignored him and walked over to the passenger side door and opened it wide. He leaned in and looked under the seat. When he saw nothing with which he would normally use to incriminate the pair, he grunted and patted the floorboard carpet fully expecting to find something concealed underneath.

The passenger and driver watched him and continually looked back at one another. They knew it was only a matter of time until they had been discovered.

"Well, well, well!" Phelps called, feeling a distinguishable lump in the carpet. He dug his fingers under the inner-most edge and yanked it up, discovering the small plastic baggie laying on its side. "What have we here?" He pinched the plastic ends in his fingertips, turned around and held the bag of coke aloft for them both to clearly see it.

Phelps laughed and stood back upright. When he turned to face them, he held the baggie up in the sunlight. "Looks like cocaine to me, boys!" He opened the top of the bag and dipped his pinky finger inside. When he retrieved it and tasted his finger, he nodded his head. "Hmmm, tastes like cocaine, too!"

"What the hell?" the driver shouted. "I know my rights! Your career is on the line now, mister!"

"You don't have any rights," Phelps barked as he hurriedly walked right past them.

"What?" the driver pleaded. His protest fell on deaf ears.

"Can you believe this asshole?" the passenger asked his stunned accomplice.

The young men watched in awe as the dirty cop strode back to his cruiser. He opened the door, climbed inside, and plopped down in the seat. He then brought the bag in his hand up to the dashboard and proceeded to pour out three, clean, even lines across its length.

"What the hell's he doing?" begged the passenger.

"I think he's doing our blow, dude," replied the astonished driver.

Phelps fished inside one of the zipped inner-most pockets of his black laptop case on the floor and withdrew a small straw. He leaned forward, smiled at his cuffed perps, inserted the straw into his right nostril and snorted the entire line. Phelps winced at the stabbing pain in his nose that came shortly afterward, closed his eyes and shook his head. "Ah, God damnit."

The passenger grunted and struck his friend with his elbow. "Well there goes his evidence."

The driver whipped his head around, concerned about what really mattered. "Where did you stash... *the money*?"

"I ditched it in the trunk," he swiftly replied. "The corrupt cop didn't even look in there."

Phelps snorted the second and last line into his left nostril and leaned his head back for several moments. He then said, "Oh, dogie." He pinched his nostrils together to block the pain and opened his eyes. He leaned out the window and said, "Hey! Smells like cocaine too! Yeah!"

The stunned, deflated drug dealers simply stared at him. "What an asshole!"

Phelps flicked a switch which both rewound and replayed the recording he had made of the entire conversation taking place near the front bumper of his cruiser.

"*Where did you stash the money?*"

"*I ditched it in the trunk...*"

Phelps turned his head at an angle and rubbed his chin. "Hmmm!" His eyes narrowed as he studied them. "*That corrupt cop didn't even look in there!*"

"What a couple of fuck ups."

Phelps exited the cruiser and walked leisurely back toward the curb. He towered over the young men and turned toward their car. He studied the Caucasian first who sat there unflinchingly, locking eyes with him for long moments before finally turning away to look at his friend. Phelps chuckled. He then laid eyes on the weaker, trembling Hispanic. He was shaking, either because he was scared shitless or because his adrenaline was coursing through his body like a raging river. Phelps smiled deviously and pointed both of his index fingers at them simultaneously. "Okay, Rock and Roll." Phelps cracked his knuckles. The guys reeled back in response. "Which one of you two hot shots is going to tell me where you stashed... *the cash?*"

"What cash?" The driver protested.

The passenger tried to sit up right as best he could. "We ain't got no cash!"

Phelps pointed at them, menacingly. "Don't give me that shit! Ya'll just scored a deal!"

"Yeah..."

Phelps' eyes widened and he cocked an ear. Did he just hear a confession?

The passenger winced, knowingly. "We didn't sell anything! We *bought.* And you just *snorted* it!"

"You want me to disassemble your vehicle?" Phelps threatened.

"Looks like you already started doing that," replied the cocky driver.

Phelps wheeled around. "Okay, boys. We'll do it your way!" He stopped short and turned to face them again. "It's *my way*, as you both know by now, but we'll make it look like... it's *your way.*"

He winked and continued on.

Phelps walked back to their car and withdrew the keys from the ignition. He shuffled through the many keys on the keyring as he walked around the side of the car, whistling like he hadn't a care in the world.

"I don't consent to you opening my trunk, pig!"

When he stood behind the rear bumper, Phelps jingled the keys on the ring toward the pair of sickened youth while holding the one he knew would unlock the trunk in plain view.

"What the fuck!" shouted the driver.

"What kind of cop are you?" added the passenger.

'The kind that doesn't give a damn anymore,' Phelps mumbled to himself.

Phelps grimaced. He inserted the key and popped open the trunk. After leaning inside and fishing around for several brief seconds, he unclasped a small plastic door on the inboard and folded it away.

"Woah! What's this?" he shouted, acting as if he were completely stunned about what he had found. He turned toward the perps waving a wad of hundred-dollar bills bound together with a purple rubber band.

Phelps held the money in one hand while slamming the trunk shut with the other. He turned around to face them while running his fingers through the bills. "This looks to be about five-thousand-dollars!"

The driver howled, "That's not yours!"

"Yo! Ain't that evidence, now?" the passenger added.

Phelps slapped the wad of cash against his open palm repeatedly, thoroughly enjoying the game he was playing. "Yeah," he answered. "So was the blow." He ran his index finger under his nose and sniffed loudly. "But you don't see that anymore, do you?" He grinned.

The uncomfortable feeling on their faces revealed their seething discontent.

"Well, the way I see it, you can both either go to jail and spend 5,000 dollars on an attorney, *get convicted anyway,* and do time. Or... I walk away with this wad and you get off with a stern warning."

"Fuck that!" the driver protested. "You got nothing on us! No evidence. No probable cause. No Search Warrant. Nothing!"

Phelps leaned in toward them and scowled. "Well, tough shit!" He pointed at them, menacingly, "It's not up to you!" He jammed his thumb into his own chest. "It's up to *me*! What do you two *dipshits* think of *that*?"

"I think it sucks!" the driver said. "I think *you* suck!"

Phelps laughed and worked his way behind his prey. "Well write to your congressman," he said as he started to uncuff the driver. "I usually don't let anyone off on such a grievous offense..." he continued as he proceeded to uncuff the passenger. "But since I may have violated that thing you said..." he slid the cuffs into the leather holster on his belt and pushed the two forward toward their car. "What was it again? Assessment?"

"Amendment!" the driver snapped.

Phelps laughed as he urged the two astounded young men into their car. "Oh, shit that's right, *Amendment*." When they were seated, he tapped the top edge of the door and added, "I'll have to Google that."

"Hey cop..." the driver started to protest.

"Shut the fuck up," Phelps retorted. He waved the cash before them and continued. "Now remember kids, just say 'no' to drugs."

The driver started the car and peeled out. When they were 10 yards away, he stuck his arm out the window and gave him the finger and yelled, "You fucking asshole!"

Phelps flipped them the bird and chuckled as they turned away. "Crazy fuckups."

Phelps meandered back to his cruiser and leaned against

the side door where he proceeded to count the money he'd seized. Suddenly, without warning, he felt the inexplicable feeling that he was being watched. He looked left and right and then behind him, but saw no one and nothing. He again focused on counting the money. He nearly leaped out of his skin when he caught something in his peripheral vision. He turned his head quizzically at the sight of an elderly man stepping off the curb to his left. He wrinkled his brow, because he knew he hadn't spotted him when he first surveyed the area and surveillance was one of his specialties.

The old man smiled warmly at him, a warmth he felt, strangely enough, in the very core of his being. Phelps glanced down at his shoes. He felt uneasy and he could not understand why that was. When he looked upward, he noticed the man reaching out to him, extending his hand, palm facing skyward.

"Could you spare some change for an old veteran?" he asked softly.

Phelps recoiled. He had never in his life acquiesced to a request for money, yet deep within him, he felt compelled to hand him the entire wad of ill-gotten gains he was holding in his greedy hand. Phelps felt like a force was pulling his hands toward the man and he fought the impulse with every fiber of his being. He drew a deep breath and tried to scrape the cobwebs from his mind by shaking his head rapidly from side to side. 'What the hell was happening,' he wondered?

When he decided that there was no way he was going to hand over even a single bill, he felt the tugging feeling diminish entirely. When he finally felt like himself again, he snorted and stood up straight. He examined the cash and brushed the old geezer off. "Sorry, buddy. I can't make any change. All I've got are hundreds." An expressionless stare was the man's only response, though Phelps detected a deeply profound sense of disappointment in his eyes. Even so, the man said nothing at all. He simply turned and walked away.

For the next several moments, Phelps could barely move. His eyes glossed over and he stood there in uncomfortable silence because something sat in the pit of his stomach and ate away at him as the result of the inexplicable encounter.

Detective Phelps moved that feeling away from his conscious mind to that place he had reflexively moved all such painful experiences, so as to simply survive one more day on the job. Such was the life of a cop. He had learned to disassociate himself from the things he'd witnessed or done at a very early time in his 24-year career. He had also learned how to distance himself from the people he had to interact with during such encounters. He had to view them as sub-human for his own psyche to remain unscathed.

When he looked back in the direction the man had wandered off to, he was gone without a trace.

Phelps opened his door and leaned inside. He knelt on the seat and reached for his laptop case and maneuvered the bundle of cash he was holding into one of the side pockets and tugged the zipper closed. After sliding it under the seat, he noticed the sunlight reflecting on the silver keys hanging in the ignition, but he decided he wasn't quite ready to leave. He came back out of the car, closed the door and leaned back against it to catch some warm rays on his face and take a long breath of fresh air.

He rubbed the center of his forehead for several long moments.

When he decided that it was time to move on, he was overcome, for the first time in his life... by a vision.

The detective forced his eyes tightly shut as a scintillating violet light flashed on out of nowhere in the center of his mind with even more intensity than the high-powered-flash-light he had used hundreds of times to disorient and temporarily blind the many perps he had interacted with during his time on the force. He winced in pain and lurched forward, coiling his hands into fists. Every lesson he'd learned at the police academy and every instinct gleaned from so many years on the force told him that he was under some form of personal attack. No matter what it was, he knew with every fiber of his being that he would not go down without a fight. But he wondered what exactly he was fighting against and how he could defend himself. He felt the veins throbbing in his temples and he thrust both hands to cover them and attempted to block out the overpowering sensory explosion going on in his mind. Finally, he shot open his eyes in his vain attempt to overcome the brightness inside him. "What the hell?" he screamed. Everything around him, including the trees and the houses were a blur. He snapped his eyes shut again and like a fish out of water, he repeatedly gasped for air. He used every ounce of his focus and strength and though he was successful, he felt as if they could give out on him at any moment. Seconds passed, though time seemed to have ground to a complete halt.

Suddenly, much to his surprise and great relief, the brilliant light in the center of his vision which had obscured everything else he had attempted to discern, began to slowly diminish and move away into the periphery until it seemed that he was looking at a blank old-fashioned television screen with a hazy, purple glowing outline around its edges.

Phelps stumbled back when he saw a scene begin to emerge from the center of that screen. He gripped the underside of the door handle with one hand and pressed the other open palm flush against the black, shiny door of his cruiser in preparation for yet another attack. There he stood, the confident veteran detective, completely overcome by a force which was invading his mind and he was utterly helpless to defend himself against it. And so, he waited, the fine lines around his eyes and his eyebrows twitching and contorting as the image came closer and became clearer in the center of his remarkable uncanny visual experience.

He saw, strangely enough, with astounding clarity, a mountain range, though one with which he was unfamiliar. Even with his eyes tightly shut, he reached forward with his right hand as if he could actually touch the trees in the remarkably vivid scene unfolding before his eyes. As his fingertips narrowly grazed the rain-drop littered leaves, the vision shuddered and arced unexpectedly and suddenly downward. Phelps felt strangely disoriented because from his vantage point, he was floating in mid-air, looking down toward the forest floor from above the tallest tree tops. Without warning, the scene and his awareness streaked straight down toward the earth. Phelps screamed and shot his hands forward in a futile attempt to brace himself against what was sure to be a fatal impact. Instead, to his relief, rather than smash his bones into tiny pieces, he felt a great 'whoosh' as if the ground was made of nothing substantial at all. He found himself experiencing streaks of scintillating colors as he was burrowing effortlessly down through the moist soil, the energizing, life-filled roots of the trees and the thick, cold mountain stone. The scene careened left and right and left again until he came suddenly through the cold embrace of the stone into a warm, artificial, subterranean metal room.

Phelps lurched back and slammed himself against the side of his Cruiser. His jaw popped open and he clutched the sides of his head. There, in his vision, as impossible as it would seem, stood a gigantic mass of corded muscle. It was human-shaped to be sure, yet its skin was like no human skin at all. It was a deep shade of green and covered in a fine scale... like some giant man-serpent by all appearances. When he could take not a second more looking at the ghastly thing, the scene seemed to pan away to reveal, in greater detail, the layout and contents of the room, including—the other occupants.

The detective shot his hands open and clenched his jaw tightly shut. His defensive mechanisms kicked into high gear when he saw a screaming, lacerated fair-skinned woman, in her early twenties, securely bound to a metal gurney, screaming in agony as two more Reptilians poked and prodded her with cruel metal instruments. Phelps groaned deeply. Even though he knew in the core of his being that he was a corrupt cop, hell-bent on abusing his power and presumed authority whenever it suited him to reign in the scum of the city whom he knew were dirty, the part of him that was still good and honest wanted nothing more than to burst into that room and attack the trio of otherworldly things with everything he had to muster. Nothing else mattered. How could it?

The closest of the three Reptilians swung its great arm downward at a 45-degree angle and swatted the woman in the side of her face, tousling her wavy, blood-streaked blond hair to the side. The shock of the blow, if she were not held down, would have blasted her clear off the table. It growled in a deep, guttural tone which made the hair on Phelps' arms stand on end. Then it spoke, in a language which was completely foreign to him, yet somehow, some way, he clearly understood every word it uttered.

"She's useless. If she knew anything, we'd know by now!" The beast glared at her without the least bit of empathy through black narrow slits in the center of its golden eyes. It snarled at her with contempt, and then at the two subordinates standing obediently nearby. Through its jagged opalescent fangs, he commanded, "Get rid of her! And report to the Overlord immediately!"

The others quickly and reflexively sprang into action. One wheeled around and swooped a scalpel off the metal tray on the adjacent table. The other moved in and pressed its hands over her. The first placed directly over her pounding heart. The second secured firmly over the top of her head. The look of anguish on the woman's face wounded Phelps in the deepest recesses of his soul. He recoiled as the woman pleaded for her life. The cacophonous, frantic screeches echoed off the metal walls.

"Goddamn you!" Phelps roared. He flexed his arms and pectoral muscles, feeling as if he were bound in heavy chains.

The woman issued one last, desperate wheezing whelp before the creature sent the blade into her soft flesh and cut a thin, clean line across her jugular. Her eyes widened as a crimson tide flowed through the wound with each last beat of her throbbing heart. The vision then faded away completely.

"No!" He shouted. He hung his mouth open in sheer agony. Then, the muscles around his chiseled jawline fired continuously until his entire face was contorted and his expression was one full of sheer, unadulterated rage. Spittle rolled off his teeth and down the corners of his mouth and chin as he grieved for the woman and his inability to help her. He spun around in a slow circle, as if doing so would allow him to change his perspective completely.

"Why?" he bellowed into the air. He could do nothing but sob. 'Would there be nothing more?' he wondered. 'Would there come any clues he could put to use in some way to bring that woman justice?'

Then the vision returned. Feeling as though he might have been given a second chance, Phelps drew a deep breath, calming himself so he could focus intently. Maybe, he surmised, he was being shown all of this for a reason. Again, he reached out as if he would be able to interact with the crystal-clear scene that he was seeing. The vantagepoint through which he was observing, hovered just slightly above and behind the shoulders of the lead Reptilian as it waved its hand over a series of glowing arcane symbols on a deeply-set, dimly-lit panel protruding from the wall. Phelps squinted, using his detective skills to narrow his focus enough to devote every millisecond to remember the precise lines of those symbols should he ever have the opportunity to interact with them personally at some point in the future. His eyes moved from side to side under his loosely-closed eyelids as he etched them into his subconscious mind.

The thick, ornate metal door slid silently into the floor, exposing what appeared to be an extra wide corridor flanked on each side by rows of small metallic cages stacked three high and extending for as far as the screen would allow him to see. 'What the hell are those cages for?' he asked himself.

Phelps then focused his attention on the images flowing through his mind as clearly as they would be if he were watching a high definition movie on his home television screen. He rocked forward and back and he looked left and right as he caught the sounds of screeching and wailing... *children.* He twisted and turned to see, and then he realized, much to his utter shock and horror, that the screams from those precious young ones were coming from *inside the cages.* His eyelids fluttered and tears began to well up and overflow out of the corners of his eyes. Tiny, bloodied human hands reached out and coiled around the bars as the thing began walking past. Then he saw one of their faces, gazing out through the bars and quivering in what he knew to be absolute terror. The Reptilian extended its powerful arms and hands and swiped the bars of the cages with the cruel, twisted claws at the ends of its fingers which forced the children's hands back into the dark confines of the cages in unison. Phelps flung his knee forward and rammed his heel back into the door panel of his car behind him in protest.

"Where the *hell* is this?" he shouted toward the sky at the invisible forces which had invaded his mind. "*Why* am I seeing this?" he continued. He was instantly overcome with sadness and sorrow because of the fact that he had never in his entire career successfully rescued a single child from the clutches of those who sought to do them harm. And worse, still, it brought back all of the terrible memories of his own childhood, when he was unable to save his very own brother from the intruder who broke into their own home late at night when they were just children. "So help me, God!" Phelps wailed, tears streaming down his cheeks. "I will tear them limb from limb, if it's the last thing I do!"

The violet colored edges of the screen in his mind flashed repeatedly until the vision was gone.

Chapter 3

HIDDEN DEEP WITHIN the jagged stone faces of the Swiss Alps, in an impenetrable fortress far below the prying eyes of the surface population, the two Reptilian officers passed through a series of dimly-lit corridors like a whispering breeze.

After weaving their way through the twisting, labyrinthine base, they turned down a long, descending, dead-end corridor and at that end, rather than striking a solid wall, they passed effortlessly through what they knew to be nothing more substantial than a hologram, a security measure, which to any of the many slave races under their control, and even the humans working alongside them, would appear unyielding and impassable.

Once through, they stepped into the hidden, damp stony embrace of a base far deeper, more ancient and more akin to the Reptilian's native habitat than the shared human base built above it, centuries later. This was a world of nameless nightmares, of secret alliances and treacherous conspiracies which could exist only while protected in the cool embrace of perpetual twilight.

The great chasm was made of shimmering dark gray diorite, naturally-embedded with millions of flecks of smoky quartz—affording the area an unremarkable, dim hue which was far easier on their otherworldly eyes than the unnatural illumination used in the many shared bases above.

Here, in the secret world below the busy, bustling surface, were caverns both great and small with ceilings of heartless stone where no winds blew, save for the slight currents rising off pools of molten magma far below and where silence and foreboding filled the dank, stale air.

The caverns themselves were connected by perilous, winding courses devoid of the life-sustaining rays of the sun, host to constant temperatures and unvarying darkness. Roughly-shaped, wickedly sharp stalactites and stalagmites filled entire chasms like the great maws of some hibernating, preternatural beasts waiting patiently to consume anything that would dare venture close enough. Shimmering pools of brackish water dotted the landscape and the only distant sounds to be heard were the constant echoing drips of water from somewhere nearby but from a place seemingly always out of reach.

The eight-foot-tall Reptilians stopped suddenly before a sheer chiseled rock face with a great black, perfectly round void dominating the center. Within moments, a bright, humming, pulsating orange sphere made of pure plasma slipped effortlessly through the opening and approached them silently. Without the slightest bit of trepidation, the officers stepped through the outermost energetic boundary of the sphere as it hovered there. The artificial intelligence responsible for its control saw to it that the occupants were phase-shifted directly into the center. The autonomic inertial dampening field system secured the passengers and allowed them to interact as they normally would, even though the sphere whisked into the void faster than the blink of an eye and instantly accelerated to transluminal velocities.

Instantaneously, the pair was transported thousands of miles into the Appalachian Mountains in the Continental United States of America, and directly into the massive control room and the monitoring station within, where one of the most ruthless, winged, white Draco Overlords monitored its human resources both within the many underground Reptilian bases and on the surface world with incalculable precision.

Lord Lahniffpsi traced his ancient, crooked, pale forefinger along the uppermost edge of the metal chair facing the pulsating crystalline monitor panel which consumed the entire wall. The impossibly-sharp hooked claw carved a deep, even gash across the chair's length, leaving a neat even pile of tiny metal filings at the end.

The tall, lanky, gray-skinned slave from Zeta Reticuli seated in the chair, shuddered violently at both the sound and the soul-shattering reverberations throughout its spindly upper back and thin, long neck. Though it belonged to a subjugated race which almost completely lacked any form of empathy themselves, and which rarely expressed even the slightest emotion, tiny beads of pearl-colored perspiration oozed out of the thick, leathery flesh of its overly-large, bulbous bald head and rolled down the side of its tiny, almost undistinguishable nose. Like water on oil, it slid effortlessly past the rapidly expanding and contracting tiny slits which functioned as nostrils until it slowly collected and gathered at the outermost edge of his ever-downward-slanted, scowling mouth. The perspiration sat there for what seemed to be an eternity until it slowly seeped into the crease between its taught lips. The bitter, aluminum taste reminded it of the one terrible truth it had learned, quite by accident really, that would haunt it for all the remaining days of its life.

Worse than feeling the cold, calculating, dominating presence of the Overlord lurking behind, was the knowledge and understanding that the extraterrestrial, interdimensional Reptilian being was absorbing, or more accurately, consuming the fear energy that was being emitted, for that very energy was now, as it had been for millennia, the most sought-after and satisfying, life-sustaining ichor known within their innermost circles as '*Loosh*.'—the cast-off, extra-low energetic vibrations of terror-stricken, rape and torture victims.

As if that wasn't enough to cause one's heart to fail, the Grey then caught the Overlord's hideous reflection in the immense black glass crystalline monitor.

Its overly-large milky-white, muscled cranium supported two even rows of small, dreadful horns which originated from just past the egg-shaped black slits on the edges of its snout, and grew in length and breadth as they wound their way up and over its forehead. There, six great hooked horrors arced back at 45-degree angles appearing as if they were cutting into the very ether around him.

Lahniffpsi sensed his slave's large black almond-shaped pupil-less eyes regarding him, so he sneered, exposing his wickedly-sharp, serrated fangs which protruded along the entire length of his tightly-pursed scaled maw.

"Focus your attention on your task at hand, wretch!"

The Zeta slave could feel the threatening claw mere centimeters from its throbbing jugular and the rest of its frail, exposed neck which was host to, by now, at least a dozen healed, once-terrible gashes inflicted by that very same mortal instrument each and every time he had failed his task master in some fashion. Though the wounds themselves had one after the other scarred over, the traumatic encounters when dealing with the Overlord, or its psychic attacks, would never truly heal.

An emergency klaxon sounded throughout the control room and a wizened elder Zeta seated at a great console before the central monitor sprang from its chair, shrieking and waving its thin arms forcing everyone to turn abruptly in its direction.

"Speak!" demanded the Overlord.

Through the overhead comm system, the multidimensional language and symbology translator relayed the being's every word and inflection. "Proxima Centauri just flashed!"

Lahniffpsi roared in defiance, smashing his clawed fist on the top edge of the chair and crushing the metal there into a dented wreck. This startling news shook him to the foundations of his core, though he was able to mask his fear behind his more formidable persona. His cruel tone was deadly serious as he extended and coiled his serpentine head around to regard the Zeta.

"Compute the distance to Earth and extrapolate the time it will take to strike!"

"Calculating," replied his loyal servant. His thin, spindly fingers worked feverishly on the laser-etched glass hologram that appeared suddenly before him. After but a moment, he continued, "Proxima Centauri is a mere 4.24 light years away from Earth. It could happen in... days."

Dismayed, Lahniffpsi replied, "And so, it begins!" He skulked around the room, his great, bare, three-toed feet slapping against the shiny obsidian floor. "Our doom is upon us! If we do not adequately shield the planet from the incoming light energy, then *everything* we have worked so hard for through the millennia... *will be lost!*"

"Your orders, Master?" came the nearby call.

Lahniffpsi careened around to face the faithful human flag admiral who had served him well throughout the years. "We can cut the flowers from the garden to prevent them from blooming, but we cannot stop the Spring from coming!" He shot his arm forward and pointed at the mammoth monitor. "Get me a visual, Admiral!"

Admiral Malldrake sprang into action and went swiftly to the console. "Relaying the stream from the Vatican Observatory LUCIFER device now, my Lord."

"Is the LUCIFER device functional?" he barked.

"It is, Master!" The Admiral snickered when he thought about the public relations story which revealed to the spoon-fed masses that the chilled device's acronym meant: <u>L</u>arge <u>B</u>inocular <u>T</u>elescope <u>N</u>ear-infrared <u>U</u>tility with <u>C</u>amera and <u>I</u>ntegral <u>F</u>ield Unit for <u>E</u>xtragalactic <u>R</u>esearch, when it was actually a device attached to a telescope in Arizona, named after none other than the Devil himself, whose name meant 'Morning Star.' He and only a few others in the highest echelons of the secret government knew that the placement of the observatory and the installed device were specifically designed as an early warning system used to identify the locations of the nearby Suns once they began to flash—events they knew would be the harbingers of doom for the extraterrestrial enslavers.

The screen periphery shifted and moved, replaying the captured video from the telescope which, by design, had automatically rotated toward the stellar event just as it had occurred.

The blank screen came to life and the room erupted in a brilliant golden light, 1,000-times brighter than that one particular sun that had flashed. Every being in the room recoiled and attempted to shield their eyes before they were fully overcome. To the Reptilians, whose eyes preferred near total blackness in their underground facilities, the intrusion of such radiance came in a blinding rush of agony. Due to their proximity of their natural Sun, the Grey's natural, internal secondary eyelids aptly closed to protect them from the glare, but the humans, including Admiral Malldrake turned their faces away from the screen and cried out in anguish.

The Reptilian Overlord moved closer and clutched the console where he defiantly stared directly into the monitor. He sneered, despite the stinging pain the light caused him. Without shifting his focus whatsoever, he growled, "What's the status of our grid?"

"Stable, Master," replied a lesser Reptilian bending over a blinking holographic panel. "We are holding at 98 percent."

Lahniffpsi's eyes narrowed and shifted to regard that very panel. "Is that sufficient to deflect the incoming wave of light?"

The Reptilian officer passed his hands over the panel and instantaneously, a holographic Earth erupted out of a black, columnar dais in the center of the great chamber. A bright red grid circumnavigating the entire planet flashed repeatedly. "Of this I am certain, Master."

The Overlord's anger became more clearly apparent as each second passed. "98... percent?" He unfurled his great bat-like wings, wings which as a species had long ago atrophied to the extent that they could never support their immense weight, but were instead used as a symbol of power and prestige. His eyes glowed like cinders in a fire. "I know you are aware of the consequences of failure!"

The Reptilians in their chairs, cowered at their stations in response to the threat and swiveled around in unison to regard him. One stood, nervously and said, "Of course, Master. It would..."

Lahniffpsi bellowed, "It would *what*?"

The officer recoiled and sank back down into his seat. "It..."

"It would mean the end of your control over humanity!" shouted Admiral Malldrake, still rubbing his eyes with the forefingers and thumb of one trembling hand, trembling due to the searing pain in his eyes and the very real fear of a ruthless response from the Overlord which at any moment, could snuff out his life in an instant rage-induced out lash.

"That and more, human!" Lahniffpsi boomed. "When the light energy causes the chain-reaction we expect it to, not even our Lord Yaldabaoth will be capable of thwarting it." He turned on his heels and stormed across the room. His upper maw curled, exposing his teeth. "Tighten the grid!"

"But, Master..." whelped one of his Reptilian operators. "That would mean diverting power from our North American grid!"

The elder Zeta nodded, its black, soul-less eyes reflecting the light from the rotating holographic Earth in the center of the room. It waved a long, spindly three-fingered hand over the globe and spun it around so that the North American Continent came into view. Rather than speak audibly, the great veins on each side of its head throbbed and moved, revealing that it was using its innate telepathic abilities to with which to communicate instead. The trans-dimensional translator cued in immediately to relay his very thoughts.

'The people of North America, given their history of disobedience, must remain subdued. Full power from the grid over that continent **must** *be maintained to avert even the slightest possibility that they could awaken in sufficient numbers to thwart our plans. Our full resources must continue to be deployed to ensure that they remain a conquered and vanquished populace. They* **must** *remain asleep.'*

"Ours now, is it?" the Overlord cackled. "Remember your place, servant." Lahniffpsi's forked tongue shot out of the narrow gap between his pursed, segmented lips. "The methods which we employ here are identical to those we used on each of your own home worlds to accomplish the same thing we are attempting here. You, as an entire species, were deprived of your own Ascension..." Lahniffpsi came up behind the elder Grey and coiled his clawed fingers around its pathetic, miniscule, withered neck. "...So that you and your people could never escape *our... grasp!*" He squeezed suddenly and forcefully. The Zeta's eyes popped open as widely as they could, nearly consuming its entire angular face. "Once the solar flashes fail to shift humanity's collective consciousness outside of this third dimension, we can deal with those who have awakened from their millennia-long slumber." He loosened his grip and ran his open hand over the crimson-hued holographic fence surrounding the Earth. He issued an order without shifting his gaze. "Put the False Tunnel of Light Matrix on screen."

A Reptilian nearby turned his attention to the console before them and within moments, a swirling white vortex appeared equidistant with the moon on the opposite side of the planet.

"Once we snuff out their lives, the trouble-makers will be drawn to the light like moths to a flame. It is there that they shall be stripped of their memories and forced back into new bodies, bodies we have shunted for eons, where they will continue to serve us throughout all eternity, never coming to realize their true power and potential."

"As it has been decreed," replied the Ancient Grey.

"Deflecting the light energy is our first and highest priority. Reroute power as needed to bring the grid to full capacity!"

Chapter 4

RAIN CLOUDS CREPT slowly across the mid-day sky. As he sat at a traffic light, a lingering thunder clap rattled the windows in Danny Phelps' Corvette, forcing him out of his daydream. Though still profoundly disturbed about the strange events that had unfolded earlier in the day, he was determined to follow through with his promise to attend the annual ritual that he and his family had taken part in to commemorate the anniversary of his brother's untimely murder.

Each year when he'd pass by the wide, rusting wrought iron gates, he promised himself that it would be the last time. Each year, he asked himself, just before taking that turn into the cemetery, how many more times could he endure reliving the dreadful events in his mind. The guilt he'd harbored for not leaping into action quickly enough to help save his brother, and the memories that would come flashing back into his mind, year after year, ate away at him like a pervasive cancer that could be temporarily stayed but never quite completely cured. Yet, somehow... something deep inside him continually convinced him to attend the annual memorial, despite his reservations.

Phelps moaned as he cut the wheel and turned slowly into Oaklawn Cemetery.

For several long minutes, the car rolled by the endless stone memorials which honored those who had once walked among the living and who had left their mark upon the world before their lights were snuffed out like a candle's flame. Danny became lost in the emptiness of it all. His brother's light was extinguished at the tender age of 13 and thus never had the opportunity to shine much at all. For he, like so many others, had fallen victim to the whims of the far too numerous cold-hearted killers walking freely among the innocent.

When he spotted his parent's and sister's cars ahead, in the distance, Phelps noticed the knot which had usually grown in his throat each and every time he closed the distance.

Phelps pulled over until his right-side tires were on the grass. He shifted into First and sat there momentarily with the engine purring, gazing into the rear-view mirror, noticing the fine lines around his eyes, noting that even though he was growing older and wiser, he had somehow been unable to free himself from his inner turmoil. He turned off the engine and climbed out. He closed the car door slowly and drew a deep breath of the crisp fall air. A light misting of rain fell lazily from unseen heights and he tightened the black leather jacket collar around his neck and headed toward the gathering 80-yards-deep into the heart of the cemetery with his head hung low. The grass fell gracefully under the weight of his black boots and then sprang to life again, as he continued on toward his family gathered around his brother's memorial.

Once he arrived, he noticed his sister Sandy kneeling beside the headstone, arranging the usual bouquet of flowers she'd brought with her. Their father—tall, salt and pepper-haired and barrel-chested—was running his index finger under his nose and holding his slender wife tightly against his shoulder with the other. They turned to regard their son who maneuvered himself in front of them both and wrapped his arms around each of them. Sandy stood and smiled when she saw that her brother had arrived. A single tear rolled down her face. She sniffled and moved into her brother's extended arms for a strong and protective, much-needed embrace.

"Let's pray," their mother encouraged, somberly.

Nicholas Phelps extended his open hands toward his wife and to his son.

Danny took his Father's hand, looked him in the eyes and turned to face the gravestone. Sandy took her brother's other hand in hers. She raised and kissed it before wrapping her other hand on top, squeezing tightly. They bowed their heads together momentarily until their father began the ceremony.

"Heavenly Father, we ask for your blessings this day to be poured upon our beloved Alex and upon those of us who remain here to grieve his tragic loss. We pray that you comfort and console us all and that we, someday, will all be reunited and dwell in Heaven with Christ Our Savior, forever. Amen."

"Amen!" they are recited in unison.

The family stood there silently, holding hands in a line for three full minutes.

Finally, Phelps' father broke that silence, with his powerful and learned voice.

"Walk with me, Son," his father encouraged.

Danny and his father broke off from the group and moved together slowly toward the horizon.

Danny slid his free hand into his pants pocket and said, "This isn't getting any easier, Dad."

"I know, Son," Nicholas nodded. He fought the tears welling inside his eyelids, but he had learned from his mother that it was far better to cry and let the emotions out than to keep them locked inside to fester.

"Your brother would have been 50 today."

"Yeah."

"It feels like it happened yesterday."

Danny sobbed and drew a deep breath. He held it as his eyes glassed over. "I feel..."

Nicholas grasped Danny's arm, urging him around to face him. "Don't, Danny. I know what you're feeling. You do this every year. We've gone through enough. Don't punish yourself."

"But I *could have...* saved him, Dad," Danny offered. "If only I hadn't..."

"You saved your sister from that sick predator—and yourself as well. Always remember that!"

Nicholas stared at the tips of his shoes. "God damned human traffickers!" He grimaced. "Child killers! I pity Satan when they show up in hell! At least he didn't suffer for long, Danny."

Phelps nodded and wiped away his own tears.

"There are no easy ways to understand this damned thing." Nicholas looked up and brushed a tear off the side of his cheek and turned toward his son. "How's the Melissa case going?"

Danny shook his head from side to side. "Not good, Dad." He felt the all too familiar rock in his stomach when he thought about his career and the meaning of it all. "Dad, I have yet to solve a missing-child case." Danny winced. "Oh, God, no matter how hard I try to let it all go, I feel like I'm responsible, ya know?"

"I know, Danny."

Danny grunted. He looked back at his mother and sister holding one another by the gravestone.

"They say time heals all wounds. How many more years have to pass by before this guilt lets up?"

"It's time to let it go, Son."

"I miss him so terribly!"

"I know, Danny, we all do."

Nicholas and Danny Phelps walked slowly and solemnly back toward the gravesite. They said nothing more at all of the incident. The time together and the silence did much to relieve them of their anguish.

Danny leaned in and kissed his sweet mother on the cheek. "I love you, Mom."

Lisa burst into a smile and hugged him as tightly as she could. "You take care of yourself out there on the streets, Danny. There isn't a day goes by that I don't worry about you risking your life and limb."

"The streets are like a second home to me, Mom," he reassured her. "I'll be just fine," he nodded. His mother squeezed both hands on either side of his cheeks and smiled brightly. He let the tears trickle down his face until he leaned forward as he always did so she could kiss him on the forehead.

Sandy came in for a final goodbye hug and the four walked off silently, hand in hand toward their cars.

Later Detective Phelps rolled along slowly through the downtown streets of Austin. The police scanner and all calls from Dispatch were unusually silent. The day had already taken its toll on him and so, as much as he wished he wouldn't have to, he began to recall the circumstances that led to his brother's murder...

* * *

In the twilit hours of early morning, 11-year-old Danny Phelps and his 13-year-old brother Alex slept soundly in the twin beds of their shared bedroom without a care in the world. Beau, their black Labrador snored softly at the foot of Danny's bed. As soon as Alex's bare feet hit the floor, however, Beau's ears shifted and moved in that direction. Danny heard the noise too and rolled over in his bed to see what was going on. His hair, in places, was sticking straight into the air and he tugged away the collar of his pajamas which had wound uncomfortably close to his neckline as he had tossed and turned earlier in the late evening.

Alex plodded toward the door, scratching the back of his head.

"Where are you going?" Danny whispered, quizzically.

Half asleep and without even looking back, Alex replied, "I'm thirsty!"

Alex opened the door as softly as he could so as not to make any noise that would disturb the rest of his family. He'd already awoken his younger brother, but it was almost impossible not to. Their grandfather had been heard on more than one occasion boasting that Danny always had the ears of a fox and the nose of a bloodhound.

Once Alex had left, Danny smirked, looked down, reached over and traced a finger along Beau's snout. Beau's eyes opened slowly and the two regarded one another affectionately. "You're such a good dog, Beau. I love you." Danny patted Beau's head. "Come here, boy!"

Beau rose slowly to overcome the hours of inactivity. He crawled toward Danny, curled up next to him and nuzzled his head under Danny's arm. The human and canine friends soon drifted off together into the soft embrace of sleep.

Several moments later, Beau's ears, ears far more sensitive than Alex's, perked up. Then Beau's eyes shot open and he turned his head sharply toward the door. A low, rumbling growl reverberating throughout the dog's chest forced Danny out of his brief slumber.

Danny rubbed his left eye with his palm and asked, "What's a matter, boy?"

Beau simply stared at the door and growled even more intensely. He jumped down off the bed and walked up to the door. His eyes glistened against the nightlight as he tilted his head from one side to the other.

Danny watched and listened, but he could hear nothing out of the ordinary. He glanced over at the alarm clock in the corner. It was 2:22 am. Beau was still reacting to something though, so Danny flung his blankets off and stood. Beau looked back and panted. He opened the door with his snout and when he had enough room, he crept out the door and down the hallway. Unsure what was going on, Danny followed him with trepidation toward the great room.

As the dog progressed deeper into the center of the house, Danny moved in cautiously from the living room and stepped onto the cool ceramic tiles of the kitchen. Beau's growls intensified, forcing Danny to quicken his pace into the darkness where he then heard faint, muffled screams. He flapped his hand against the wall in search of the light switch when Beau suddenly began to growl more violently.

Danny listened to the scratching sounds created when Beau dug his claws into the knotted pine planks of the great room floor and sprang into the darkness, baying wildly. When he finally found the switch he'd been searching for and turned it on, his eyes grew wide and he found himself completely and utterly paralyzed with fear at the inconceivable scene unfolding before him.

* * *

An explosive blast of a nearby gunshot snapped Phelps back

to present day. He shook his head and hit the intercom. "Delta Papa to Ocean One. You copy?"

The monotone voice coming from Dispatch erupted immediately. "Copy, Delta Papa."

Phelps hit the accelerator and scanned his surroundings as he sought the perpetrator. "Shots fired at Congress and Seventh." He scrutinized the alleyway. "Requesting backup!" He cut the wheel tight and careened into the alleyway. Yellow fast food wrappers and white paper cups caught underneath the car whisked away behind it as the car screamed ahead. Phelps squinted and saw a lone figure slumped over on the pavement, reeling in obvious pain. Phelps slammed his foot on the brakes and engaged the emergency lights. Phelps winced when he saw the victim. "Officer down, 10-52!"

The radio squelched. "Copy 10-52 Delta Papa. Medics en route."

Phelps scrambled out of the car, made his way over and knelt just short of his convulsing colleague. He heard the police scanner come to life as emergency services personnel coordinated their response.

"Hold on, soldier! Medics are on the way!"

Though he was writhing in pain, the officer struggled significantly to speak. "Two of 'em..." He gasped. "Hispanic male... mid-20s, black shirt..." He spat up blood. "Blue jeans... armed." Phelps whipped his head around trying to identify their avenue of escape. The wounded officer continued. "White male... mid-20s, bald, white T-shirt, blue jeans..."

A crowd began to gather around the entryway to the alley. Phelps moved through them as he approached the street and scanned the crowd until he spotted a man who fit the description of the second suspect. He tore after him, speeding up when he saw the youth look back and break away into a sprint.

Phelps ran as fast as he could while shouting after him, "Freeze!"

The crowd grew thicker and Phelps deftly maneuvered around and in-between the people on the sidewalk. The looks on their faces revealed their shock when they discovered the crazed burly man bearing down on them so rapidly.

Phelps' eyes never lost sight of his target. The suspect skirted down another alley and jumped a fence ahead of him. 'Damn, he's quick!' Phelps thought to himself. Phelps continued, undaunted.

"I'm gonna get you!" Phelps taunted. He was intrigued by the fact that even though the perp was clearly half his age, he was actually closing on him, and closing fast. "I'm gonna get you, goddam it!" Phelps accelerated. "I'm right behind you!"

The suspect zipped around the corner onto Congress avenue and actually picked up speed, but Phelps would not allow the punk to win. '*Not this time.*' Not after so recently reliving the thoughts of his brother's murder. He would never... as he closed the distance... allow someone to get away with something like that again. '*Never again,*' he thought to himself. As if time had in some extraordinary way, came to stand still, Phelps was unexpectedly upon the suspect in a flash. As Phelps leaped into the air and dove on top of him, the young perp lunged at him in mid-air with his elbow and struck Phelps cleanly in the side of the jaw. The men clutched one another as they descended toward the blacktop.

Two squad cars, with their emergency lights flashing wildly, screeched to a halt as both men rose to face each other. Phelps smirked. He knew, that despite the age difference, his professional training gleaned from both the police academy and from years studying Shotokan karate gave him the upper hand. The young man swung wildly. Phelps ducked and maneuvered himself around to his side and quickly completed the route behind him, where he forced him into a full nelson and slammed him flush against the nearest squad car. He pressed his powerful arms in together snugly to squeeze the willpower out of him.

"I got you now!" Phelps shouted. 'That was almost too easy,' he thought to himself.

"You pig!"

"Now what are you going to do?" Phelps' grip tightened as he waited for a response. None came. Finally, he wailed. "Huh?"

From their squad cars, the uniformed policemen leapt into action and Phelps shoved the suspect into their custody. One officer spun the perp around and pinned him against the squad car while his partner handcuffed him. He went right to work reciting his Miranda rights verbatim. "You have the right to remain silent..."

Phelps rested his hands on his hips and to begin calming himself down. He laughed in the face of the perp. "I got you, goddam it!"

One of the Officers patted Phelps on the shoulder. "Nice work." He noticed the gash in his shirt caused by the fall. "Detective, if you don't mind, we'll take it from here."

Phelps pointed his finger at the suspect and then turned to face the crowd of nervous onlookers. "He didn't think I'd get him." He beamed pointing his finger at the perp. "I got him, ha!"

By the look of their facial expressions, several onlookers found Phelps' antics amusing. Others clapped and cheered.

The police officers eased the suspect into the back seat of the squad car. He sulked and sent his head back into the rear head rest several times, likely contemplating the serious repercussions of his actions.

After the reports were recorded, the ambulance had left with the wounded officer, and they had finished with their official duties, the two arresting officers slid into their patrol car and began to pull away. Out of nowhere, Phelps jumped in front of the car, forcing the officer who was driving to brake suddenly. Phelps leaned over and slammed both open palms against the black-painted hood of the cruiser while locking eyes with the passenger in the left-side rear seat. The officers shook their heads and rolled their eyes, respectively. After Phelps moved out of the way, the car passed slowly by, and as it did so, Phelps rapped on the window with his knuckles to ensure that the perp was looking directly at him. "I told you I was gonna get you!" He then smiled at him with a maniacal grin. "You fuck-up, I got you!"

The car moved off slowly as Phelps stared the perp down as he was looking back through the rear window. Phelps extended his arm and hand in a simulated handgun fashion and pointed it at the suspect who have him a wide-eyed, angry look as the exhaust fumes rose slowly into the autumn sky. Phelps turned toward the crowd, who had, by and large, dispersed to go about their own business. All but one man, directly across the street staring intently and directly into Phelps' eyes.

Phelps squinted as he studied the man. The clean-cut businessman held a briefcase securely by the handle and looked on with an uncomfortably expressionless gaze. '*Where have I seen you before?*' he pondered. The man simply refused to move. Phelps looked away and then it hit him. It was the man he'd encountered earlier: the old man who asked for a handout. '*You again.*' he said to himself. "*Who the hell are you?*" They glared at each other for a moment, then Phelps looked away to contemplate.

When he looked back, the man was nowhere to be seen. Phelps stood there, frozen and though he could not understand why, he was suddenly realizing that he was embroiled in something far outside of his comfort zone or understanding.

Minutes later, Phelps shrugged and headed back through the alleyway toward his cruiser. The day was only half over, he knew, but he wondered what more it had in store for him.

Chapter 5

THE GLOWING NEON signs of the Lonestar Gentleman's Club flashed brightly in the late overcast morning, and to Danny Phelps, they could not have been more alluring. Phelps tucked a manila folder under his arm and headed for the front door. Just when he'd reached for the door handle though, he noticed a hunched over, translucent figure out of the corner of his right eye, opaque and if it were standing erect, Phelps surmised, it'd be nearly two feet taller than himself. Phelps whipped his head around and saw nothing. This was a disturbing pattern becoming all too familiar. He followed the front of the building until he turned the corner. He peered into the alley and saw no sign of anybody. Phelps stood there for a brief moment and ran his hand over his head, a coping mechanism he'd learned from watching his own father throughout the years. He paused briefly and cupped his palm over his neck and squeezed tightly.

Phelps skulked over to the front door, depressed the thumb latch and swung the door open wide. The bar was dark and it took a moment for Phelps' eyes to acclimate before he could see exactly who was inside and where they were situated. It was a product of his training, something he couldn't help himself from doing, as annoying as it was when he was off duty and simply needing to relax. He paused in place momentarily until he could see properly.

Neddo, the partially deaf Hispanic bar back nodded and

smiled at Phelps as he was busy polishing the glassware
from behind the bar, joking around with Chaz Dawg, the
35-year-old Jamaican detective wearing his native dreadlocks long and authentic enough to blend in on the street,
yet well-groomed enough to satisfy his professional role as
a detective and Danny Phelps' partner in crime. After such
a long and emotion-laden day, Neddo's contagious laughter
was a welcome sound indeed.

"Yo, mon, Danny, check 'dis shit out," Chaz called out, beckoning him closer. He tapped the counter in front of Neddo
to get his attention. "Neddo! Neddo, mon." Neddo looked up.
"Tell Danny what you just told me."

Neddo shrugged his shoulders and frowned. He pointed
toward the tanned-skinned, athletic erotic dancer with slender legs, long, thick black hair and eyes as blue as a teaspoon
in the Mediterranean.

Phelps turned briefly and saw the beautiful young woman
completing a circuit around the dancer's pole in the center
of the stage which reflected the light from the spinning disco
ball overhead. He raised a brow. He knew that when there
were no patrons interested in table dances, she'd do her pole
routine.

Neddo smiled and lifted his chin up as he did so. He winked
and said with his slight speech impediment, "I think she likes
me."

Phelps coughed loudly. "Terra?" he replied, twisting his
wrist around and pointing at her with his thumb. "You..." Phelps
continued, "actually believe... you have a snowball's chance
in Hell... with that fine woman on that pole over there?"

Neddo nodded, confidently.

Phelps could stare down anybody, and win, they all knew,
and this time was no different. In fact, his intense gaze could
stop traffic if need be. He placed both hands on the counter,
one each on opposite sides of the folder. He looked at his

friend Chaz and then back at Neddo and studied his breathing and his facial expressions, most specifically the frown lines in his forehead and his pupils. Then he studied his hand placement. An uncomfortable silence sat heavily over the area like a thick, dense, heavy fog.

Finally, a full minute later, Phelps turned toward his partner with a coy smile and admitted, "He *does* actually believe it."

The guys laughed in unison as Phelps regarded his folder on the bar top. Phelps grimaced, for all to see and when he lifted his gaze, he locked eyes with Neddo and said confidently, "Too bad she digs me Neddo." Neddo stepped back, discouraged. "So... good luck with that." He snapped his head back to Chaz and rapped his knuckles on the counter. "Where's Luke?"

Neddo thrust his head toward the restroom. He shuffled his other fist up and down over his groin area.

The trio burst into fits of laughter. Each voice was unique and overlaid one another perfectly to create what they all truly felt was a beautiful music they performed together as the close friends that they were.

"Speak of the Devil," Phelps jeered, as they spotted Luke coming around the corner. Luke smiled as he approached and when he came within range, Phelps slapped Luke on the side of the arm and squeezed his bicep tightly.

"Yo, boys," Luke shouted. "What brings ya'll in here so early?"

"You feeling all better there, big dog?" Phelps replied.

Luke winced.

"Taking good care of yourself, are ya?"

Phelps and his friends shared amused glances. It was an inside joke if there ever was one and the object of that joke still hadn't caught on.

Luke frowned. "I'm... fine."

"I bet you are," Chaz added.

Luke looked thoroughly confused. "Bourbon?"

Phelps nodded. "You know me too well, my man. You know me too well..."

Chaz and Neddo's riotous laugher were one thing, but their knowing glances forced Luke to slam the bottom of the bourbon bottle onto the countertop and the noise startled Phelps, too.

"What the *hell* is so funny?" Luke prodded. "Every time I come out of the bathroom..."

The three men doubled over and laughed continually.

The laughter receded. "Luke," Phelps asked.

Luke pursed his lips and wrinkled his brows.

"How many cops does it take to throw an inmate down the stairs?"

The bartender poured the bourbon into Phelps' glass. "I don't know, Danny," he huffed. "How many?"

"None!" Phelps countered. "He must have tripped." Phelps grinned as the three men burst into laughter. Phelps slammed his drink.

Chaz pointed over toward an isolated area of the club. "Let's grab a table, mon."

Phelps scooped up his folder, jammed it under his arm and snatched his glass in time for Luke to pour another. He winked at the bartender and moved away before he could say anything clever.

The two detectives walked over to a secluded corner table and sat down.

"How'd it go with your boys?" Chaz asked, his glassy dark brown eyes studying him intently.

Phelps set his drink down on the table. "Sweet," he replied, grinning from ear to ear. "Like taking candy from a baby. Easiest five-thou I've ever made."

Chaz cackled, "Cool, mon!"

Phelps set the folder down on the small round black-mirrored table.

"Dat it?" Chaz asked. Phelps had promised to show him something that would peak his interest.

Phelps nodded and opened it up. He drew a breath and said, "Just another couple of fuck-ups. Tim Pasetta, 42—did two on a four-year money laundering sentence and a couple of misdemeanors here and there." He flipped through the pages. "Look at this ugly spud..." Phelps showed his partner the photo of the scowling, broken-nosed degenerate. His face was acne-scarred and deeply pitted.

"Damn, mon," Chaz said, recoiling. "I didn't know dart teams have goalies."

Phelps paused a moment to consider what the hell Chaz just said, elected not to comment and simply took a drink before continuing. "Hector..." he put special emphasis on the first name. "...Esparza, 38. He had two assault convictions and got a year for selling to an undercover cop. That's it."

"No mob connections?"

Phelps looked over the top edge of the page and gave Chaz a knowing look. "I'm telling ya, brudda." He always enjoyed mimicking Chaz's accent. "Easy pickings."

Chaz flashed his golden teeth. "When's it goin' down?"

"Esparza scored the deal already. No busts yet, either."

"Nice," Chaz said, sucking on the soggy end of a used toothpick. "Now dey gotta clean it."

Phelps nodded, downing more of his drink with a quick flip of his wrist. "Right."

"What's da drop date?"

"Don't know yet. Still working on it. They usually have their pow-wows on Tuesday nights. We'll wrap it up then."

"What if Tuesday don't work for dem?"

Phelps set his glass on the table. In an imitated Jamaican accent, he replied. "No worries, mon. Got my scanner to record it all." He chuckled to himself when he saw Chaz's broad smile. "You running anything?"

Chaz shifted his eyes and checked out the bar to make sure no one was listening. "You'll love dis. Ever hear of da Bible Bandits?"

"Kind of new on the scene, aren't they?"

"Check it out. Dey hit up three banks in Houston; two in Dallas and dey just hit one in San Antone."

"Oh yeah!" Phelps nodded. He slapped the table surface with his open palm. "They quote scripture on the job."

Chaz laughed. "Disguise demselves as Biblical characters, too."

Phelps joined in on the shared laugh. "Yeah, I like their... style." He became suddenly serious. "What about them?" He took another swig.

"Dey just hit dis bank in San Antone dressed like Catholic priests."

"That's funny. I always knew they were shady."

"I'm pretty sure I know who dey are."

Phelps frowned, waiting for more information.

"Chris Evans and Jake Simmons."

"Yeah, right. And you know this how?" Phelps pressed.

"Rex, my former partner and I busted dem six years ago before I transferred to APD. Dey were doing mini marts and liquor stores. Dey did four on a five-year sentence."

"Yeah," Phelps continued. "So, what makes you think it's them?"

Chaz became agitated, as if he needed to explain himself further. He winced and shot his hand forward. "Cuz, mon!" he shouted. They looked around them to see if anyone had noticed the outburst. Chaz lowered his voice as he leaned in towards Phelps. "My ex-partner called me. He's assigned to da case. Wanted to know if I had anything to help him out. A witness heard one of da bandits say, "Do exactly what I say or you'll be *a long time dead!*"

Phelps angled the corner of his mouth down sharply. He then repeated the statement silently, moving only his lips. He paused and looked up at his friend. "That's a weird thing to say."

"Right. What I said, mon. Who talk like dat?"

"I still don't know why you think it's Evans and Simmons."

"Dat what da witness heard six years ago."

Phelps finished the sentence for him, "You'll be a long time dead."

"That's why they're gonna get busted," he whispered to himself. Phelps was incredulous but continued to listen.

"Didn't tink anything of it at da time... but when Rex mentioned it," Chaz continued. He bounced his extended arms around and added, "...déjà-fucking-vu, mon."

"If you're not gonna bust 'em, what's in it for us, seriously?"

"Dey hit banks when vaults are open. In dose few minutes, dey in and out."

"When's the armored truck on the scene?"

"Four o'clock in da afternoon, on da money." Chaz chuckled, flashing his golden teeth again.

Phelps pursed his lips. "How much are these guys planning on getting away with?"

"About $100K."

"That's it?" he snorted. "Sounds risky as hell for $100K!"

"We wouldn't be robbing da bank, mon!" Chaz shot his hands in the air. "We'd be robbin' *dem*!"

Phelps snatched his glass, downed the last small sip of his bourbon and slid the glass toward his friend. He then peeled back his black leather jacket sleeve and checked his

Rolex. "I dunno. Broad daylight? Security cameras? What else you know 'bout these guys?"

A group of new patrons gathered around a nearby table. Phelps caught that same blurred shadowy figure he'd seen earlier out of the corner of his eye disappear right through the solid front door like a summer breeze would blow through a screen door. Phelps did a double-take.

"What the... ?"

"What is it?" Chaz asked.

"Something really crazy is going on."

Chaz gave his partner an unsure look.

"Let's get out of here."

Chaz shook his head from side to side. Phelps was already half way to the door before Chaz stood and rushed to catch up with him as they exited the building. They walked in opposite directions toward their cars when Chaz turned around. "Hey, Danny!"

Phelps turned around and extended his arms to his side, palms facing skyward. "You talkin' to me, punk?"

Chaz pointed at him, taking that challenge and then some. "Deir next hit..."

Phelps opened his mouth in anticipation.

"...is Austin!"

Phelps let his arms fall to his sides to make as much sound as possible as they slapped against his sides. He then spun on his heels and continued toward his car. Without changing course, or glancing back, he shouted, "Who gives a shit!"

Chapter 6

THE NEXT MORNING, with a steaming cup of hazelnut coffee in one hand and a half-eaten ham, egg, and cheese croissant in the other, Phelps walked slowly across the wide parking lot toward police headquarters. Within moments, Chaz was walking up behind him as briskly as possible with his own cup of coffee in his hand, quickly enough to catch him, but not quite fast enough to spill it over the rim. Then Phelps saw him approaching in his peripheral vision. He contemplated their earlier conversation concerning those damn Bible Bandits. He saw right through the many ways he and Chaz could get caught in this caper. Chaz always had good intentions, but he could rarely close the deal. Chaz was like the younger sibling always looking up to his older brother, eager to learn more. Phelps whipped his head around.

"What'chyu 'tink 'bout our discussion?" Chaz queried.

"Those Bible Bandits?" Phelps replied, turning his head slightly to regard him.

"Fifty grand each, mon!"

Phelps turned fully around to face him and shot him a scornful glare as he held his hands up to his sides. "Downtown in broad daylight? It's way too dangerous." He dropped his arms down to his sides. "It sounds like they'll be going down soon anyway." Chaz watched him as he shoved the last bite of the sandwich in his mouth and flicked the crumbs off his shirt. "And..." he grunted, crushing the paper wrapper into a ball in his hands and holding it in his clenched fist. "I don't want to be around when they do." Phelps zeroed in on Chaz's cup and sniffed the air around him. "Man, that smells better than the light-roast crap I've been drinking. What is it?"

"You like, mon?" Chaz replied. "You haven't had real coffee 'til you've had Jamaican beans."

Phelps rolled his eyes and grinned. "Here we go again." He wrapped his arm around his buddy as they walked toward the doors. "I've never met a man who was prouder of his heritage..."

"Fresh, aromatic, dark roasted beans..." Chaz continued. He cupped one hand before himself and said, "Beautiful, big-breasted women hand-picking dem from..."

"Okay, I get it!" Phelps interjected. He arced back and whipped the crumpled sandwich wrapper into the metal drum sitting beside the door. He raised a victorious fist into the air as if he'd just made a three-pointer as Chaz opened the double-metal blue doors of the building.

Once inside, they walked slowly down the long hallway toward the conference room.

"So, what're we gonna do about dis, mon?"

"Let's focus on Pasetta and Esparza," Phelps replied. "Less work for both of us. It's way more profitable too. More stealth. And..." Phelps said, widening his smile. "More fun."

Chaz smiled and nodded approvingly.

Phelps continued, "I don't wanna be bending over dollars to pick up pennies."

Chaz shot him a petulant look. "What?"

"Know what I mean?" Phelps finished, tossing his coffee cup into the nearby trash can.

"No!" Chaz challenged. "I have... *no idea*... what you mean."

Phelps opened the conference room door and the two

men took seats next to each other. The chatter of two dozen detectives filled the room.

Chaz whispered, "Crazy white boy and his crazy-ass sayings."

Phelps chuckled and said, "Come over tomorrow night. We'll see what they're up to..."

"Nice Z06 ya got, Phelps!" Detective Harris called out. Phelps whipped his head around. "How come you're the only guy on the force driving something so choice?"

Phelps mocked Harris with a broad grin. "It's brand new too, Harris."

Harris sat on the edge of the chair, stirring his cup of coffee. "So, what's up with that? Where are you gettin' that kind of green?"

"I moonlight with a paper route, Harris."

The room erupted in laughter.

"Funny Phelps, all kidding aside, just how do you afford it?"

The Chief paused while writing on the dry erase board preparing for the meeting.

Phelps then focused on the man who was rapidly becoming his nemesis. "It's called solving cases, Harris. You should try it some time."

"Woah..." jeered the others in unison.

Phelps raised his arms and waved his hands to quell the raucous crowd. "Maybe if you solve some, you won't have to get a ride to work from your mommy every day."

Harris scowled. "That's my *wife*, asshole."

"Hmmm," Phelps mused. "Thought you were gay."

The room erupted in laughter. Harris just sneered and mouthed the word '*asshole*.'

"Yo, listen up, people!" The burly African American police chief said as he approached the podium and leaned in closer to the microphone. When he saw that several of the men were still engaged in conversation, he shouted. "That means shup up, ladies!"

Phelps looked around at the other detectives and said sibilantly, "Yeah ladies."

The chief opened up a folder and he strained to read the paper inside. He grunted and slid on his glasses. He glared at Phelps over the rims for several long seconds and finally shot him an annoyed look. "Last night, we had a 187 near the corner of Chicon and Eighth around 2300."

Several of the officers groaned.

"Looks like some psycho drove an ice pick into a transient's dome."

"Where does anyone get an ice pick these days?" begged one of the older detectives.

"Another cockroach bites the dust," said another.

The chief pointed a threatening finger at the audience. "Who just said that?"

The men shifted in their seats and looked around at one another.

"He's another low life we don't have to worry about and we all know it." The chief's eyes bulged. "But... talk like that is something that'll come around and bite us all in the ass, so it doesn't need to be said aloud, *ever*. Not in *my* department! Do you hear me?"

"Loud and clear," Detective Harris shouted.

Phelps rolled his eyes.

"Okay then!" the chief retorted. He cleared his throat before continuing. "The victim was found in an alley beside a dumpster with the murder weapon stuck in his head."

Chaz turned sharply to regard Phelps. He responded only by shifting his eyes toward him and then back again to face the chief. "Sounds like someone I know..." Chaz whispered, jokingly to his friend.

Phelps shot him a rage-filled, momentary glance.

"Sorry, mon."

The chief simply shook his head. "Shoe prints led to and from the scene. Forensics is all over it. We also have a witness who says he saw a blue '68 Chevy Camaro at the alley's entrance at approximately the same time. He peeled off his reading glasses. "The witness didn't see the driver arrive or leave. There are no other details. There can't be more than a single '68 Camaro in Austin. Let's get on it. And remember..."

Phelps yawned.

"Yo, Detective!" the chief shouted.

Phelps was turned toward Chaz discussing something which caused several of the officers to snicker.

"Phelps!"

"Yes, Sir!"

"Am I boring you?"

"Oh, God. You have no idea..."

The room erupted in laughter.

The chief scanned the room. He traced a threatening pointer finger at several of the men. "Shut the hell up, people. Goddam it, Phelps!" The chief pressed his glasses in tight against the bridge of his nose. "You know what, Phelps?"

Phelps raised a brow.

"Despite your recklessness, you've solved almost every case you've ever had."

"Almost," Harris interjected.

"Phelps interrupted. "Thank you, Sir!"

"Shut the hell up, Phelps! I'm not finished." He pointed at him sharply.

The chief's massive biceps bulged, as did his enormous pecs. "You two piss me off, you know that?"

Phelps chuckled and looked down at the desktop.

"Congratulations!"

Phelps didn't like the sound of that. He slowly glanced up at the sour-faced chief.

"You just earned yourself this case. Way to go, smartass!"

"But, Sir!" Phelps pleaded. I'm already working on the missing child case!"

The chief clutched both ends of his lectern and squeezed firmly in yet another display of his musculature. His white shirt looked as though it would come apart at the seams.

"Oh yeah?" Harris interrupted. "How is little Melissa anyway? What line of bullshit false hope are you feeding her parents this week?"

"Shut up Harris!" the chief barked.

That lit a fire inside him that soon erupted on his sullen face. The chief looked firmly at Phelps. "No bullshit, Sir! Her parents submitted a sample of her DNA to forensics."

"And?" the chief asked, quizzically.

Phelps gave him a disturbed pale stare immediately afterward.

"God damnit, Phelps! This Melissa case is high profile. That's why you're on it. I want *results* and I want them *yesterday*! Got it?"

Phelps closed his eyes as he nodded. He knew, that everyone was well aware of the fact that given what he'd been through, the missing child case type was something that was very personal to him.

"Dismissed!"

Indiscernible chit-chat ensued as the others began to file out of the room.

The chief shouted. "Remember, people. Watch your six!"

Phelps and Chaz were the last to slip through the door. When they began walking down the hallway, Phelps stopped short when he saw Harris turn around to face him and break into a song. Phelps' eyes widened when he heard him singing the lyrics from Pat Benatar's song, Suffer the Little Children:

"Sweet Melisa, I hope your suffering was brief..."

The words were like steel hooks tearing into Phelps' heart.

Harris was taunting him, luring him, even beckoning him into a confrontation that had been building for a long time.

Chaz didn't fail to notice Phelps' look of sheer distress. He had never seen his partner so terribly affected like he was at the moment. Each syllable Harris sang looked as if Harris himself had jammed that ice pick mentioned in the meeting right into his heart.

Chaz was caught off guard when Phelps lunged toward Harris. "God damn you, Harris!"

Chaz fought to hold him back by extending his powerful arm in front of Phelps' chest. "Take it, easy, bruddah."

Phelps fought him to get closer to Harris. "You goddamn asshole!"

Chaz jacked Phelps up against the wall. "Don't let him get to you! You're stronger den dat!"

Harris spat on the shiny black tile floor.

"You're better den dat!"

Restrained, though seething mad, Phelps watched helplessly as Harris walked away down the hall. Without even looking back, Harris flipped Phelps the bird just before he turned the corner. Once he was out of sight, his voice echoed off the concrete cinder blocks of the walls, "Fuck you, Top Cop! You ain't shit, after all!"

Phelps roared and fought to get free, but Chaz held him securely in place for his own good.

"Why do you even listen to dat asshole?"

Phelps maneuvered himself out and away from Chaz's grasp. "Get off me, goddamn it!"

Chaz released him. "Dis case you're working is seriously messing you up, mon." He pointed toward his own temple and spun his finger around counter-clockwise. "You need some help?"

Phelps looked down the hall and slowly but surely regained his composure. "I'm good."

"You sure?"

Phelps exhaled forcefully. "Let's just wrap up Pasetta and Esparza!"

Chaz nodded. "Okay, mon. Calm down, bruddah."

Phelps eyed him.

"Calm down!"

"I'll see you tomorrow night."

Phelps slinked away.

Chaz called after him, "Pasetta and Esparza are da least of your problems, mon."

Phelps shook his head and jammed open the exit doors. The lyrics he'd heard Harris sing haunted him when the rest of the song came to mind:

Sweet Melisa, I often think of you, every time I hold my baby in my arms...

The distraught detective moped through the parking lot until he reached for the door handle of his Corvette. Then, he saw her, a little brown-eyed girl holding a Teddy bear, hand in hand with her mother across the street. He stood there motionless. The girl locked eyes with him. More of the lyrics boomed in his mind:

I say a prayer for your mama and daddy, too. Every mother's nightmare, when will it ever end? Suffer the little children... at the hands of evil men...

* * *

The next evening, in the great room, overlooking Lake Travis, Phelps was leaning over his pool table about to make the next shot when he heard footsteps approaching outside. He looked around him, tightened his grip on his pool cue and scooped up his cocktail glass from the edge of the table. He turned down the music so he could hear more clearly. There came a series of five solid knocks on the door. The door swung wide and in walked Chaz Dawg.

"Yo, mon! How's my Anglo-Saxon bruddah?"

Phelps grinned from ear to ear. He was actually pleased to see him. "My Jamaican bruddah," he said, extending his arm in an inviting manner. "Enter dis dwellin'."

Chaz came right in and went straight to the bar.

"Pour yourself a drink!"

Chaz glanced over at the table and focused his attention on the police scanner.

Both Detectives knew it had already been carefully tuned to Pasetta's frequency and he was waiting impatiently for the call.

Chaz poured a drink for himself. "Any word from our boys?"

Phelps swirled the bourbon around in his glass with a subtle hand movement. "As a matter of fact..." Chaz stood upright, staring ahead at the wall. "I picked them up earlier today. They're... negotiating."

"Cool," Chaz replied, turning around. He took a sip of his drink. "How much are we talkin'?"

"About one and a half mil..."

Chaz coughed in his glass, set it down and quickly wiped his mouth. Then, he whipped out a joint. "Sweet, mon! He lit the joint which crackled as he drew a long, slow, deep drag. "Half mil for da laundry."

Phelps leaned on the pool cue. "That's what I figure. With a few kickbacks, I think we'll walk away with a half mil each." Phelps flung the pool cue in the air, which he then caught with cat-like precision. He then leaned in and shot the Number Three Solid.

Chaz extended his arm.

Phelps imagined what it must be like to become lost in the effects of the dimethyltryptamine. He imagined looking at his friend in a cloud of white smoke who became nothing but a blur. The dreadlocks made him look like one of those otherworldly creatures from… 'what was the title to that movie?' he thought to himself. He nodded we he'd found the answer. 'Predator! That was it.'

Chaz put his hand on his hip, wondering what was going on in his friend's mind "Mon, you okay?"

Phelps narrowed his eyes to act like he was flying high. "Oh, wow… man!" Like this is really… far out, man!"

Chaz laughed so hard, he coughed. His lungs were likely as black as his skin by now.

Phelps grabbed his alcoholic beverage instead. "C'mon, Brudda!" You know I don't smoke that shit."

Chaz lifted another pool cue out of the rack securely fastened to the wall. He took it in both of his hands and bent over the table. "Never tried it?" Chaz clearly couldn't fathom it. "Ever?"

"Once," Phelps quickly admitted.

"I knew it! Everybody tried it, mon!" He cackled.

"When I was 16," he continued. His eyes glassed over momentarily. "My sister and I got high together."

With a sharp 'crack,' Chaz shot the Four ball into the pocket. He glanced over at Phelps. "And how was it?" Chaz took another hit.

"We shared a quarter pound of dry dog food together thirty minutes later."

Chaz belted out, "Oh, shit! Dat's nasty, mon. How did dat shit taste?"

"De-fucking-licious."

The shrill call of the telephone triggered the police scanner.

Phelps turned the music off. "Hold on, it's our boys." Phelps and Chaz moved in closer and listened intently as Phelps turned the dials.

The thick New York accent they heard came from none other than Tim Pasetta talking into his cellphone. "Yeah?"

Esparza replied. "Clean?"

"We're cool. Just to be clear, my cut is half a mil?"

"I'm good with that," Esparza agreed.

"Okay, listen up. You go buy a membership at The Tri-athlon Club."

There was a long, silent pause.

"That key I gave you... It's my locker, Number 47. On Sunday, get there around 9:00 PM. They close at 10, it'll be dead. I'll be there a few minutes before you to make the drop. Bring a black gym bag full of clothes, or whatever."

"Those lockers secure enough?" Esparza challenged.

"They're solid."

Esparza huffed. "Big enough for that much cash?"

"Don't worry about it!" Pasetta retorted.

"I'll be there."

The phones both went dead and the scanner went silent soon afterward.

Phelps beamed. "Intercept at the gym!"

"No shit! Don't want to screw wit dese dudes if we don't have to. Only problem is, it's a tight window, mon."

Phelps paced the room, deep in thought. He rubbed his jaw and chin when he came to an abrupt stop. "Yeah. Couple of minutes max. I'll go to the club tomorrow, get a membership and case it. I'll bring my gym bag with what I need inside." He pointed at Chaz. "You follow Esparza to the gym. I'll keep my eyes trained on Pasetta. Timing will be the key!"

"No shit, mon. Get in. Make the switch. Get da hell out!"

Phelps pressed his thumb deep into the center of his opposite hand and massaged it, excitedly. "Let's grab some cash!"

The two corrupt, money-hungry, conniving cops grinned as Phelps racked the pool balls in preparation for a real game as Chaz turned up the volume knob on the sound system.

Chapter 7

DETECTIVE CHAZ DAWG'S hands worked furiously over the computer keyboard at his desk as he ran a search for the makes and models of the vehicles owned by Pasetta and Esparza. Phelps walked up from behind making just enough noise so as not to startle him.

"Anything?" Phelps asked.

"Check it out," Chaz replied, jamming his index finger into the glass monitor. "Esparza's got himself a new ride, a Black '19 Cadillac Escalade."

"Nice," Phelps said. "Hope we don't cause him to miss a payment."

Chaz laughed. "How did the gym go?"

"Piece of cake. Locker room's secluded. Security cams non-functional. Number 47 has a lock on it. It looks like a typical padlock, so there shouldn't be any problem."

"So, he was dere?"

Phelps nodded. "I saw him."

Chaz pointed to the images on the computer screen. "Look familiar?"

Phelps raised an eyebrow. "That's our boy." Phelps started to turn away when he spun around and smacked Chaz on the shoulder with the back of his hand. "Hey!"

Chaz looked up at him.

"Let's hit the club tonight. Make sure we didn't miss anything."

Chaz nodded in approval. "Cool."

* * *

Later that evening, inside the Lonestar Gentleman's Club, the music was thundering and the business was booming. Phelps was seated at a small cocktail table with Chaz and a slender, young, cool, and calculated Chinese man who liked to go by his Americanized name: Johnny. 'Funny,' Phelps thought, that two of his most trusted compatriots didn't even go by their real names, but by aliases instead.

Terra, the voluptuous exotic dancer sashayed over to Phelps and sat on his lap. "Hey, Danny," she purred. The timbre of her voice always sent chills up his spine. "I haven't talked with you in a while." She smiled when she felt the growing girth in his jeans and leaned back, wrapping her arms around the back of his neck. She began to undulate against him. Phelps eased her up and she quickly spun around and straddled a single knee. She ran her hands over his chest and shoulders. "Wow, Danny! You been working out?"

Phelps was a bit taken aback by the size and feel of his harder than usual muscles. "Hmm, well, I haven't been hitting the gym very hard, maybe it's all the action I've seen lately..." Little did Phelps realize that the light which had struck his body earlier was altering his DNA and was restoring his body into the perfected human form it was encoded to be. This was yet another obvious sign that something beyond his understanding was taking place right before his very eyes. Something that now others were witnessing as well.

Terra smirked at him, coyly. "Danny Phelps," she squeezed his collar snugly in a playful manner. "Do you have eyes for another girl?"

Phelps chuckled. "Not a chance!" He inhaled deeply and relished the seductive scent of her perfume. He then ran his hands over the tops and sides of her shoulders. "Mm, girl. You smell nice."

Chaz and Johnny eyed their partner and decided to let him enjoy some down time, rather than think of something wise or clever to turn his screws as they all so often do to one another whenever they have an opportunity.

When Phelps slid his fingers in a little too close, a corner of Terra's mouth turned down and she snapped, as delicately and firmly as possible, "C'mon, Danny." She looked around to make sure no one was keeping tabs on her. "You know the rules around here..."

"I thought *you* made the rules, girl."

Terra swiped Phelps' hands away from her inner thigh. "Rules are rules, Danny. So, cool it!"

Chaz and Johnny exchanged amused glances and did their best to conceal their laughter.

"Come on, sweetie." Phelps grinned. "I thought you liked me."

"I do like you, Danny, but not when you're drunk." She turned around and sat on his lap with her back toward him.

Phelps guffawed. "I'm not drunk," he insisted. "Well... not *that* drunk." He turned to his buddies, winked at them and asked, "Hey, all ya'll..." He slurred his words, revealing the obvious. "Am I drunk?"

Chaz leaned over the edge of his chair ever so slightly and asked Johnny, "You tink he drunk, mon?"

Johnny pinched his thumb and index finger together with a slight space in between them. "I'd say, he's half-drunk."

"What da hell is half drunk?"

"Have you ever been fully drunk?" Johnny queried.

Chaz frowned. "What'chyu tink?" he shouted.

Johnny grinned from ear to ear. "Okay, then. Half of that." They both roared in hilarity.

Phelps ran his hands up Terra's back and around her

shoulders and then back down again, squeezing her slender waist. He snuggled close and pressed his cheek against her mid back and he held her tightly against him.

"C'mon, Danny!" Terra roared. "Knock that shit off."

"Oh, sweetie," Phelps protested, hugging her more powerfully. "Be a sport." He reached up and fondled her breasts.

Terra quickly propelled herself off, wheeled around and slapped him in the jaw with enough momentum to force his head around toward his wide-eyed friends. They hooted and howled as Terra pointed a threatening finger his way. "Goddamn it, Danny!"

"Look like homeboy's get'n de shit kicked out of him by a chick," Chaz boomed.

Johnny chuckled. "Looks that way to me. Never seen a chick beat the shit out of this dude before."

Phelps pursed his lips. "Bullshit!" No chick can beat up any man. It's physically impossible."

Terra set her hands on her hips and shot daggers at him with her look of pure disdain. "I can kick your sorry, drunken ass faster than you can say assault and battery, Detective."

Chaz and Johnny teased Phelps in unison, "Oooo."

Phelps let his head slink down to the side, so he could shoot her an angled, upward, challenging glance. He had just about enough of her mouth. "You can't kick my ass, Terra."

"Wanna see me?" Terra scowled, threateningly. She held her first two fingers tightly together and shot them toward him to emphasize her point.

Phelps laughed. "But Terra, you're just a girl."

Terra repeatedly shook her fingers at him. Her face was now flushed and she drew in deep breaths through her nose and exhaled forcefully.

Phelps challenged her again with his widely-drawn eyes.

Chaz reached over and patted him on the shoulder. "Yo, mon. You'd better back off."

"You're such an asshole, Danny!" She spun on her heels and stormed away to a nearby table while flipping him the finger.

Phelps leaned in toward his friends. "Asshole?" Phelps splayed out his legs in front of him and leaned back in the chair, so that the back side of his neck rested against the top of the low rising velour chair. He stared at the black-painted ceiling and became lost in the spinning of one of the many fans overhead. His head began to spin with it.

Johnny studied him while tracing his pointer finger up and down the side of his temple. "You need to work on your moves, buddy."

Chaz nodded. "No shit, mon. Have his moves ever worked?"

"Not even close."

Phelps called out. "Terra?" There was no answer. "TERRA!" he bellowed.

"What?" came the shrill, distant call.

Phelps smirked and his friends laughed. He closed his eyes and fantasized about her. "Will you call me an asshole again?"

Chaz and Jonny burst into laughter.

"Fuck you, Danny!"

Phelps fought to maneuver himself up and over to grab his cocktail glass. When he leaned over his chair close enough to see that his glass was empty, he raised it into the air and looked around. "Oh, shit!" he moaned. "Ya know, boys. The service around here sucks!"

Chaz and Johnny were stunned when Phelps, having some inexplicable sudden surge of energy, leapt straight out of his chair and stood before them like nothing had happened at all. They were even more startled when he clapped his hands together and said, nonchalantly, "Alright, boys, this round is on me." He eyed Terra coyly and began to shimmy over toward her.

She held her open palm up toward him when he drew near. "I'm very angry with you, Danny."

Phelps pushed her to her limits but he knew she liked him and he approached her anyway. Confidently, Phelps took a seat near her. "You are?"

Terra maintained a calm, assertive stance and looked directly at him. "I am, Danny!"

"This is anger?" Phelps inquired. He gave her a look like a puppy gives when it learned it had done something wrong. "I like you, Terra. Let me buy you a drink and make it up to you."

Terra's expression softened slightly. "You're acting like a complete asshole, Danny Phelps!"

The harsh words were only bouncing off him. Terra was the most beautiful girl in the club and only he could get away with such a caper. "You know what Danny? This is why you're single!"

Phelps grinned as he knew he so loved being single.

"You can be such an asshole!"

"No, Terra," he assured her. "I'm single because I wouldn't want my life to be anything other than what it is."

Terra began to calm as she became more understanding of Phelps.

A silent moment passed.

Phelps pleaded, squeezing her hand. "C'mon, Terra, let me make it up to you. Let me buy you a drink. Anything you want."

Terra thought for a moment and then smirked when she finally came up with the solution. "Sure, you can buy me a glass of the finest champagne."

Phelps fought to bring himself to his feet and mumbled to himself. "I had to ask."

"What did you say?" she demanded.

"Nothing," he grinned.

"You know, Terra... champagne is nothing more than sparkling wine."

"I know that! You know, Danny. Most guys are dogs. But you..." she pointed at him. "You're a stray dog!" Phelps grinned at the compliment.

When he walked away, he stumbled into a misplaced chair on his way to the bar. When he arrived, he leaned into the waitress station and stammered. "Luke, buddy. A round for my boys and a glass of your finest champagne for Princess Terra."

Luke smiled from the glass rack and gave him the thumbs up sign. "You got it, Danny."

Despite all of the let downs and his drunken demeanor, Phelps actually felt pretty decent about himself and about the prospects for a fun evening among friends. He felt a slight tingle in the top of his head and abruptly turned in time to catch the fleeting glance of a barback carrying supplies to the bar. Phelps had never seen him in the club before, but his face seemed uncannily familiar as he stocked the bar. Phelps felt a growing knot in his stomach. 'Where... have I seen that guy?' he thought to himself. He narrowed his eyes and studied the man as his cool and calculating mind went to work. Then his eyes lit up like quasars. The homeless man... the businessman... and this time, a man *disguised* as a barback.

"Hey!" Phelps shouted in anger at the top of his lungs.

The barback turned to face him. "Yes?"

Phelps pointed his finger directly at him. "Who the hell are you?"

The barback seemed totally unaffected by Phelps' challenging tone. He leaned over the back edge of the bar so Phelps could make direct eye contact with him. He placed the palms of his hands on the edge of the bar and leaned in even closer. He replied softly with a resonant sound to his voice that echoed inside Phelps' core like a slow, rumbling thunder. "You know she's dead, don't you?"

Phelps wanted to step backwards, but found himself paralyzed, mesmerized. The words shook his very soul to the core.

The barback let Phelps sit with what he had just revealed and moved slowly backward toward the office. When Phelps came out of his disorientation, he coiled his fingers around a glass tumbler and clutched it securely.

"Don't you walk away from me, goddamn it," he barked. "I'm talking to you!" Phelps shot his hand back behind his head and hurled the glass at him which exploded into pieces as it struck the door.

Chaz, Johnny, and Terra exchanged dumbfounded glances when they heard the sound of breaking glass.

Luke slammed his open palm on the bar top and shouted, "What the hell's the matter with you, Danny?"

Phelps shot him a disturbed glance and pointed toward the door. "Who *the fuck* was *that?*"

The bartender reeled back in obvious dismay. He whipped a bar towel back over his shoulder and it hung there as he shouted back, "Who the fuck was who?"

Phelps couldn't believe he actually had to explain himself. He jammed a finger in the direction of the office and boomed, "That guy!" His teeth were bared by this point. "That guy back there! Who is he?"

Within but a moment, the manager stormed out from the back offices holding a clipboard with his reading glasses hanging low on his nose. He regarded the shattered pieces of glass on the floor.

"What the hell is going on here, Luke?"

Luke shrugged. "He threw a glass at door, and I haven't a freaking clue why."

Phelps jammed his threatening finger at them both and

then whipped it toward the door. "Who the hell is that guy back there?"

"What the hell are you talking about?" the manager replied.

"That guy! Back there! Who is he?"

"There's nobody back there Danny!"

"Don't you tell me... I just saw somebody go back there!"

Chaz swatted Johnny on the shoulder. "Looks like homeboy's get'n into trouble again. Let's go!"

Phelps studied the bar for a quick way to get behind it and get straight into that back office. Just as he was about to hurl himself over, Chaz and Johnny grabbed each of his shoulders and held him firmly in their control.

"Woah, mon! Take a breath!" Chaz offered.

"Yeah, Danny. Go easy!" Johnny added.

Phelps shook his arms and shoulders in their firm clutches. "What the hell's going on here? Someone's following me! Taunting me! I just saw him go back there."

"I'm telling you, Danny!" the manager reassured him. "There's nobody back there."

He locked eyes with Chaz, their mutual friend. "You'd better get your boy the hell out of here."

Phelps juked his shoulders, trying to escape as Chaz and Johnny maneuvered Phelps toward the exit door.

Phelps looked over his shoulder and then right back at Chaz. "I'm telling you... this is real. You have to believe me. I saw someone!"

"Who gives a shit," Chaz interrupted. "Let's get da hell out of here, mon!"

* * *

By the time Chaz had pulled the Corvette into Phelps' driveway and turned off the engine, Danny had already fallen asleep and was snoring softly with his head leaning back against the headrest. Johnny pulled in beside the curb, moments later. When the car came to a stop, his head slumped forward and a fine line of drool dribbled out of the corner of his mouth and began to dangle.

Chaz winced. "Gross, mon!" He fished out a crumpled napkin out of the cup holder and pressed it against his friend's face.

Phelps woke up, disoriented and mumbling to himself. "Huh?"

"Shit, wipe your slobbering face, mon!"

Phelps blew the tiny piece of paper napkin that stuck to his lower lip. "We home?"

Embarrassed for his friend, Chaz said, "Yeah, mon! Get yo' drunken ass out da car and go to bed! Take da keys, here!"

Phelps snatched the keys, fumbled with the handle, cracked the door open and leaned into it with his shoulder. He fell out onto the concrete driveway, laughing heartily. Phelps turned around and saw the neighbors' light go on inside their bedroom. As Chaz watched, Phelps stood upright and leaned in and put his finger up to his lips. "Shh!" he said, laughing uncontrollably.

Chaz closed his eyes and shook his head. "Mon, I don't know 'bout chyu."

"See ya when I see ya," Phelps said. He moved into the driveway, off balance, and though Chaz was sure he'd fall over on more than one occasion, his friend actually made it inside unscathed.

Phelps stumbled into his bedroom, tossed his jacket onto the floor, flicked off his shoes and slid right into bed. He didn't even bother to cover himself with the blankets and after he heard Chaz and Johnny drive away together in Johnny's car, he was unconscious within seconds.

Stripped of their superior abilities by the Reptilians, humans were left with only the capacity to survive... the double-stranded helix. With much of their DNA disabled and lying dormant, humanity fell into the deepest depths of lower consciousness—fear, greed, anger, envy, and self-hatred.

Chapter 8

THE BRILLIANT, RADIANT SUN rose slowly over the horizon and when it reached the tree branches outside, it shone directly into Phelps' upstairs bedroom window. As the golden rays crept closer toward Phelps and finally struck him in the forehead, he reflexively reached his powerful arm around behind him and maneuvered a pillow over his head to conceal his face. Once he was again resting comfortably in relative darkness, he tried, vainly, to drift off to the silent lucidity of sleep, but his mind became more and more pre-occupied with the vivid, disturbing images of the events which unfolded that one fateful early morning, 37 years in the past...

*   *   *

Still frozen with suffocating fear, Danny watched helplessly as Beau sank his teeth and claws into the arms and legs of the intruder who had pinned his older brother down on the floor.

At this point, Danny could do nothing but observe, still trying to overcome the shock and awe of the situation. Upon closer scrutiny, he saw that Alex's right wrist was pinned securely to the floor by the man's knee pressing his full weight down upon him. Alex strained to twist his head around towards Danny and screeched, "Danny, help me!"

Danny looked down in horror, trying to summon the courage to intervene. But he still couldn't budge.

Alex struggled, quivering under the weight and pressure of the man's legs pressing down against him. Alex's free arm thrashed wildly about with every ounce of strength he could muster. Alex's look was one rapidly descending into a look of sheer desperation and terror.

Suddenly and surprisingly, Alex brought his fist up and cracked the man in the jaw with a solid left-hook, forcing him to come up slightly from his low bend. Beau's snarls filled the room as he let go of the man's shoulder and instead began to rake at his back with his claws.

Ignoring the burning pain of the dog's cruel claws, the man growled himself, continually batting the dog away.

Danny's heart nearly burst through his chest each time he watched his dog relentlessly fight to go in for more, only to be knocked away.

Meanwhile, upstairs, in the master bedroom, the boy's parents Nicholas and Lisa Phelps were jarred awake by the commotion. They exchanged bewildered glances, but their parental instincts forced them to fling off the covers and spring into action. Without even thinking, Lisa instinctively snatched the cordless phone from the charger on the night-stand and began dialing for help. As she did so, Nicholas leapt out of bed, ran to the door and threw it wide open. He burst into the hallway a second later, as Lisa brought the phone up to her ear.

In the living room, Danny's mouth fell agape as Beau came in again, this time high, leaping at the neck of the intruder who desperately fought to keep the canine's deadly maw from finding a hold on his throat.

Angry fires welled in Danny's eyes when the intruder swatted his dog away with a powerful backhand, but he sub-

limated them, understanding that he stood alone against a
formidable opponent.

The man sneered at him, seething with rage. Danny cautiously stepped back when he beheld the man's eyes which
were filled with a radiating wickedness, which alone seemed
capable of siphoning the life force away from him and steal-
ing it away altogether.

Still effectively pinning his brother to the ground, the
intruder moved his hand to the side and coiled it tightly
around a glistening knife hilt. Danny's jaw fell slack when
the man unsheathed an eight-inch serrated steel, black-
bladed hunting knife and brought it up before him with a
sinister grin. Before he could react, Beau leaped up onto the
man's wrist and began gnawing. The man gritted his teeth
and groaned.

A cold sweat took hold of Danny as he gazed in horror
at the scene rapidly unfolding before his eyes. 'What could
he do,' he wondered. The man was three times his size and
even his older brother and their faithful dog were unable to
subdue him. Now, in this last critical moment, the intruder
shifted his focus entirely and began to chant as he spun back
around and held the life-ending blade over Danny's helpless
13-year-old brother, who was writhing in his pajamas on the
floor under the intruder's immense weight.

As Nicholas made his way down the stairs, still unsure
about the exact nature of the disturbance going on, Danny
scanned the room for something, anything he could use to
help defend his brother. Then he spotted the glimmering
handles of the pair of his grandfather's Japanese Ceremonial
swords displayed proudly, one above the other, on wooden
mounts above the fireplace mantle. Danny knew that the
Katana was too long for him to wield proficiently, so he set
his eyes upon the shorter Seppuku blade instead. He leapt up
onto the slate hearth. As soon as his bare feet had slapped

against the cold, bare stone and once he had found his balance, he sprang upward, arms fully extended, coiled his fingers around the shiny black bamboo scabbard and yanked it off the wall. As he did so, one of the mounting brackets flew off and away from the wall and plunked down harmlessly on the glass coffee table. The other bracket swung downward, but remained securely bound to the wall as it hung loosely on a single nail. Gravity allowed Danny to come down solidly on both feet wielding the sword and luck alone landed him within perfect striking distance beside the intruder, whose sole attention was fixated upon Alex.

Nicholas froze when he spotted Beau snarling and growling as he tugged at the wrist of the knife-wielding arm of the intruder.

The man nodded gravely, accepting it as a minor inconvenience.

Nicholas shook himself free of the paralyzing fear that momentarily took hold of him, and rushed toward them. A shrill, slicing sound echoed off the limestone bricks of the fireplace and slate hearth when Danny unsheathed the wicked, curved, folded-steel blade as Beau tried desperately to stay the man's hand. Instead, the intruder reached over with his free hand and clobbered Beau on the top of the head with a closed, clenched fist. Beau whelped and let go as the man scooped his hand around Beau's chest, and flung him away with such brute strength, the dog struck the nearby wall and yelped.

Lisa Phelps burst into the great room just as the intruder drove the knife into Alex's chest and Danny simultaneously plunged the Seppuku blade clean through the man's temple and out the other side as easily as a toothpick through an olive. As the man's blood squirted out along the shining blade and onto the floor, Lisa's screams boomed throughout the room like the tolling of a great, cacophonous bell.

A wave of imparted emotion swept over Nicholas, a wave of despair and terror so great that he could not combat it. His mouth shot open in a silent scream and he staggered backward, crashing into the wall and clutching helplessly at his own chest.

"No!" Lisa wailed. The long and terrible, exasperated scream and the world-ending pain that came with it seemed to last forever.

She looked down at Alex whose face twisted and contorted in a look of both shock and pain.

"Alex!" Lisa screamed.

Danny stood there frozen. Realizing what he had done, his hands sprang open to let go of the sword hilt. Before the family's astonished eyes, the intruder teetered over like a great, felled tree, dead and gone well before his lifeless body ever struck the wooden floor with a loud 'thud.' Danny held his quivering palms before him, staring at them, frozen in blind terror at the fact that he had just taken the life of another human being and at the series of overwhelming events which had unfolded before his young, innocent eyes.

Still suffering from total shock, Nicholas yowled and did the only thing he could think to do. He reached down to his waist and began tearing off his own white T-shirt just as Danny's sister Sandy burst into the room herself. When she saw her oldest brother jerking spasmodically and gurgling indecipherably on the floor, Sandy cupped her hand over her mouth and fell down to her backside, shrieking in disbelief.

Lisa came in diving on her knees, sliding on her silk nightgown across the last few inches of the wooden floor. She scooped her arms under her son's neck and legs and pulled him up into her lap and up close to her bosom. His blood quickly found its way into the silk of her nightgown as it gushed out of his open wound. Tears rolled down her face, wrinkled and contorted with anguish as she held her baby boy snugly in her arms, rocking him gently back and forth, at the very least to try and bring him some semblance of comfort. Instead, much to her dismay, he coughed suddenly, spewing streams of already clotting blood from his mouth with each desperate gasp.

Waves of revulsion and guilt rolled over Danny when he looked at his brother's young, blood-soaked body. Alex turned his head to look at him and the sadness in his eyes and the tumult of Danny's emotions were too much for him. He could not escape from the endless, echoing of Alex's last damning words, "Danny help me!" Danny covered his ears to shut them out, but they both haunted and taunted him. Unable to find his breath, Danny collapsed to his knees in the corner, sobbing. He was visibly jarred by his father's trembling voice.

"You hang on, Alex! You hang on!" Nicholas shouted.

Alex groaned. His eyelids began to flutter and his eyes rolled back into his head.

Nicholas fell to his knees and pressed his shirt against Alex's chest, desperate to stop the bleeding. Faint sirens grew louder as the emergency vehicles Lisa had summoned earlier, raced to the scene.

Danny fell back onto his rear and held both sides of his head tightly. He wept and ran his fingers through his hair, trying to massage the pain away somehow. He failed, he thought. He failed to save his only brother, his best friend.

Outside, the medics and police cars screeched to a halt and the sounds of car doors opening and slamming shut signaled the family that help had finally arrived on the scene. But, as they all feared, it was too late to save Alex's life.

Alex lay still and barely alive in his mother's arms. He was bleeding profusely and he was reaching out gasping desperately for air. Danny sat there in total shock, looking on as Alex choked on his own blood.

Beau limped in and whimpered, licking Alex's hand and fingers as Lisa whispered into Alex's ears. "I love you, baby boy. I love you, honey!" Danny could do nothing but sob as he watched his brother fight for the last few moments of his life. Alex drew a series of shallow breaths, but with each one, more blood spewed out of his mouth. His eyes fluttered and his head finally fell back in his mother's chest as he slipped into death.

The entire family wailed together and descended rapidly into the deepest recesses of helpless despair.

Danny came in and knelt over his fallen brother. Tears welled up in his eyes and spilled over. He turned to look his parents in the eyes. "He killed Alex!" He moaned and sobbed and collapsed over his sibling's body. "He killed my brother!"

* * *

Phelps threw the pillow he was using to shield his face to the floor and opened his eyes. Sadness and emptiness fully consumed him. When he was but a boy, he yearned for the time when he'd finally come to learn the answers to his deepest and most profound questions. That time never came. Instead, whenever the demons of his past began to oppress his mind, there was no comfort to dispel them, and no solace to be found. He was no closer now to understanding the mystery surrounding the purpose of Alex's death than he was all those years ago.

Phelps wound his legs over the side of the bed, stood and wandered in a daze into the bathroom. He hoped that the hot shower he would soon slip into would somehow numb his pain.

Once he had dressed and finished breakfast, Phelps snatched his keys off the counter, locked the front door behind him and walked out into the driveway. When he turned around, there, in the sunlight, was his glistening candy apple red Corvette: his pride and joy. As he stood there scrutinizing the car, he thought about how stupid he was for drinking so much the previous evening and how he was grateful that his friends helped him home such as they did.

Phelps pursed his lips and paused for a moment.

Then, he squeezed the keys in his hand, spun around and slapped the garage door opener on the wall. The door began to roll open and when it was finally up, Phelps grinned as his black Dodge Charger Police Interceptor came clearly into view. The Vette was for pleasure, he knew. The Charger meant business. He opened the door, slid inside, inserted the key and the powerful super-charged engine roared to life. The door closed with a deep 'thud.' The onboard laptop lit up and the police scanner started chirping and squelching as Phelps turned around to look out the rear window and proceeded to back out into the street.

He studied his muscle car momentarily and hit the remote to the garage door on the overhead visor. Then, he looked out the front windshield and narrowed his eyes. It was a new day and it was time to get some answers.

After he wound his way through the rural neighborhood and moved out onto the open stretches of roadway, Phelps opened the windows, hit the accelerator and screamed through the countryside with the wind whipping through his hair.

Phelps thought long and hard about the man he had seen repeatedly, first after he robbed the drug dealers, then on the street, and finally, in the bar. He frequented the place far too often to fail to notice a new employee, associate, or even a new customer for that matter. There was no way that same guy could have just suddenly started working there out of the blue and how in the world would neither the bar manager nor the bartender not know he was back there interacting with him so? 'Who was he?' he wondered. That was the prevailing question on Phelps' mind. More intriguing, though was 'what did he want?'

Minutes later, when Phelps rounded the corner, the first thing he managed to discern was that he was swiftly approaching a large, rotating bright white sign with an over-sized red arrow in the center, adjacent to the newly-erected housing subdivision ahead in the distance. When he was about to pass by, it was as if time had slowed to a standstill. He caught the expressionless face of the sign spinner in the rightmost corner of his front windshield and it sent his emotions into a tumult. When the sign-spinner's face came clearly into view on the car's right side, the deeply-penetrating stare shook Phelps' very being to its core.

"What the..."

Phelps slammed his foot down on the brake pedal and cut the wheel. The car wheels shuddered upon hitting the thick, stone gravel and deeper sand on the side of the road and when the brakes kicked in, the tires dug deep gouges as they fought for traction. Phelps whipped his head around toward the rear window and saw the man facing him, with the motionless sign now held firmly in his cupped hands. Phelps shifted into Park, tore open the car door and leaped out. "There you are!" he barked, pointing menacingly at him. "You son of a bitch." He reached for his holster. "You ain't going anywhere. Not this time!"

The man smiled calmly and asked, "What can I do for you, Officer?"

Phelps pointed at him while maintaining his grip on his sidearm. "Put the goddamned sign down!"

"Is there a problem, Officer?"

Phelps rushed up to him. "Give me that!" he demanded. He ripped the sign out of the man's hands and flung it away from him into the grass. "You can start by telling me why the hell you're following me."

"Following you?" the man replied. "I'm not following you."

Phelps was jarred. "Don't give me that shit! I've seen you masquerading all over town wherever I go." He pointed at him threateningly. "Let's see some ID!"

The man snickered with an air of arrogance, "I don't have... ID," emphasizing the last word as if it meant nothing at all to him.

Phelps guffawed. "You don't have ID!"

The man shrugged.

"What's your name?"

The man smirked at him. "I don't have... a name."

Phelps was completely stunned. 'Can you believe this shit?' he asked himself.

"You don't have a name!" Phelps guffawed. "Did I fuckin' hear that correctly?"

The man's eyes beamed with a sudden, unmistakable inner radiance and peace that not even hot-headed, Detective Danny Phelps could deny. "I AM that... I AM."

Phelps bared his teeth. 'Goddamn it.'

The man shook his head in dismay. He seemed disappointed with Phelps' choice of words.

"I knew you were a freak!" He motioned for him to turn around. "Up against the car!" The man acquiesced and turned around as ordered. "Hands on the roof!" Phelps barked. He threw the man up against the car. "Spread em!" He kicked at his heels. The man did not protest or move in any manner whatsoever and Phelps proceeded to frisk him. After a few moments, Phelps found absolutely nothing of any substance on the man. No wallet. No watch, jewelry, keys, nothing. Not even some loose change in his pockets. He looked around the scene where he had been standing when he first found him there as he approached. He kicked the gravel and the grass nearby. There was no trace of any food wrappers or water bottles. 'Nothing,' he thought.

"How long have you been standing here?"

The man didn't answer.

"How did you know I'd come this way?"

The man smiled.

"Who's employing you?"

"Nobody." The answer came calmly and confidently.

"Don't give me that shit," Phelps continued. He leaned in over his shoulder and did his best to taunt him. "Someone's paying you to spin the fucking sign for this subdivision! Who is it?"

The man did nothing but stand there silently.

Phelps grumbled and went over into the taller undisturbed grass and found the sign, lying there face down. He reached the toe of his boot underneath and lifted it up to get a look at the information underneath. 'There had to be something with which to identify the man or his employer.' He saw nothing but a plain white surface. "What the..." He bent low and flipped the sign over with his hands until it was lying flush on its back side. The front side was completely blank as well. There wasn't even a trace of the red arrow he'd clearly seen as he approached in his car. Phelps rubbed the front of his head with his fingers. 'What in the hell is going on?' he wondered. 'What's happening to me?'

Phelps wheeled around and snarled. "Ok, what the hell is this?" he demanded. He stood slowly, coiling his hands into fists and curling his lower lip between his teeth. "You come clean, Mr. No-name, or I'm gonna lock you up!"

The man didn't move a muscle. "On what charges would you arrest me, even if you could?" he answered coldly.

"Are you shitting me?" Phelps spat. Now his authority was being challenged. He wouldn't have it. Any of it.

"You can't arrest... me."

Phelps unbuttoned his handcuff holster and tore out his shiny metal cuffs in an instant. He held them aloft for the stranger to clearly see. He dangled them so that they clinked together. "I do whatever the fuck I feel like doing!"

The man turned and cocked a smile. "I've always liked that about you."

Phelps' nose turned up into a taut wrinkle. "Alright, that does it." He grabbed the man's wrist and ordered, "Hands behind your back!"

The man did not protest and allowed Phelps to cuff him securely. He leaned in until his lips were just barely brushing the fine hairs on the back side of the man's ear. "You like that, motherfucker?" He held the 'r" as long as he could so he could exhale onto the man's face until his breath was spent. He breathed in sharply through his flaring nostrils. "You like that shit?" He grabbed the man by the chin and forced his head around to look at him squarely in the eyes. "I own you!" His eyes narrowed. "You hear me?"

"No, Danny."

Phelps' eyes grew wider than he could ever remember. 'How the hell did he know my...'

"I own... you!"

Phelps wrapped his hands in the man's shirt and turned him fully around to face him. "What the fuck is that supposed to mean?" He jacked him up against the car. "How do you know my name?"

The man smiled warmly. That radiance stunned him, precisely as his gaze did upon their first meeting.

Phelps reached around with his right hand and tugged on the door handle while holding the man against the car by the chest. He grabbed him by the arm, shoved him to the right side of the car, bent his head down, moved him into the back seat and slammed the door.

Phelps stumbled a few steps and ran his hands through

his hair again. He drew a deep breath in through his nose and exhaled forcefully. Finally, he spun around and climbed into the driver's seat, slammed the door snugly, and shifted into Drive. When he hit the accelerator, the tires kicked up the gravel until they moved onto the pavement. Once there, he increased his speed until he was cruising smoothly. When they had traveled about a quarter of a mile, he looked into the rear-view mirror and stared into the man's eyes.

"Welcome to my world, Mr. Whatever-the-hell-your-name is. Whether you like it or not, I'm going to get to the bottom of this and I'm going to start by finding out who the hell you are." He focused on the road ahead, stewing all the while in his anger and frustration.

"Indeed, you will," came the voice, three-fold more serious and more powerful than he'd ever heard the man speak before. Phelps buckled against the ominous tones.

When he recovered, even though he was still partially stunned, Phelps thought to himself, 'Can you believe this guy?' He studied the road ahead of him. Never in all the years on the force had anyone talked back to him like the man was talking to him. 'So daring and bold.'

"You listen to me!" Phelps shouted, at his wits' end. When he looked into the rear-view mirror, the man... was gone. "What the hell?" Phelps blared. He slammed on the brakes again as he veered the car to the side of the road. He cranked the shifter lever into Park so forcefully, he feared he might have caused some damage. He quickly dismissed that notion and he jumped out of the car and peered into the back seat. He fully expected the man to be lying on the floorboard. 'Where else could he be?' he wondered. When he peered in the window and saw nothing, he yanked open the door and leaned inside. He patted the seat with his open palm. There was no one. No trace. Phelps backed out of the car, set his hands on the roof and looked up toward the sky. "What the fuck?" he shouted. He then propped his elbows up on the roof of the car and sank his face into his hands. "What's happening to me?"

Chapter 9

A MISSHAPEN FIGURE shifted warily in the thick, cascading walls of white fog. Phelps knew that the man could barely see his own hand as he held it aloft and stumbled slowly forward. The sweat was rolling off of Phelps' soaked black hair and slipping down onto his smooth, saturated chest and dripping down onto his exposed, muscular thighs as he sat there quietly observing. The relentless heat and overpowering scent of eucalyptus oil began to take its toll, so he secured the white towel firmly around his waist with one hand, and slipped silently off the slick, multi-leveled tile bench and pushed open the door.

Other than the one man who had come in to disturb his brief respite, and the tell-tale sound of a single active shower in the adjacent room, the men's locker room at Triathlon Club was otherwise deserted. Phelps knew it was time to act, while the coast was clear.

Phelps worked his way to the wall of lockers directly across from the steam room where he had secured his belongings when he first arrived. The room at that time, though sparsely populated, was far too busy for him to complete the task as he had planned, but now the time was right. He opened the metal locker door quickly and tugged out a black gym bag. He scanned left and right and behind him to ensure that the coast was still clear and then walked briskly toward the other lockers, his slick bare feet slapping against the tile floor as he worked his way past the rows.

The detective quickly located Number 47 and opened a vacant locker door nearby. He slid the bag into place and closed the door. He then peeled off the soaked towel he had been wearing around his slender waist, bundled it into a ball, and tossed it into the hole in the top of the counter. He snatched a fresh towel off the mahogany shelf, dried his hair and got dressed.

Five minutes later, Phelps exited the locker room and maneuvered himself into a nearby pectoral machine, so he could use his arms to partially obscure his face as he spied on the front entrance. He spoke softly into his wireless earbuds, "Chaz... where are you?"

The sounds in the background let Phelps know that Chaz was in his car, as planned. "I'm on Esparza, a few minutes away." Phelps nodded and pressed against the weight bar grips. "Is Pasetta dere yet?"

"Not yet," Phelps replied, easing the bar upwards. He looked around and paused. "Hold on."

He spotted Pasetta as he whisked inside the front entrance. "It's him." He noticed Pasetta clutching the handles of the black gym bag tightly. "He's got the money." Phelps eased the bar in the down position. He narrowed his eyes.

"Get on it!" Chaz urged.

Phelps stood and moved from behind and through the machines to conceal himself as best he could. "10-20?"

"Almost dere," Chaz replied.

Phelps had to act even though his partner was not yet there to back him up, should things go south. He slipped into the locker room and peeked around the corner. He spotted Pasetta. He had already removed the bag that was sitting inside locker 47 and was sliding the black gym bag he was carrying inside to replace it. Pasetta closed the door and whipped his head around suddenly, forcing Phelps to duck out of sight momentarily. When he took another look, Pasetta was glancing around the opposite corner and when he saw no one around, he slid a lock from his jacket pocket and secured it into place.

"All too easy," Pasetta mumbled. He reached down to retrieve the bag he set on the bench as Phelps rushed around the corner and past Pasetta before he turned around.

Chaz's voice came through the wireless headset. "I'm in da parking lot."

A moment later, Pasetta turned the corner with the black bag tucked securely under his arm and exited the locker room. Phelps rushed to open his own locker just a few doors down and grabbed his own bag.

Just as he was about to reach in, a great 'whoosh' erupted as the steam room door opened, followed by clouds of con-cealing vapor, which provided the perfect cover for what Phelps was about to do. The morbidly obese, beet-red man waddled out of the steam room and wheezed as he tried to catch his breath. "Whew!" the man panted. Phelps focused his attention toward the shower and the sole inhabitant there. Luckily, Phelps mused, he was *still in there*. Phelps peeked around the corner just in time to be spotted by the other man.

"Shit!" Phelps' face was wrought with dismay.

The man called out toward him. "I should be used to that kind of heat. It's no more intense than the heat on a typical Austin summer day." He guffawed loudly.

Phelps slapped his bag down on the wooden bench and looked at the lock Pasetta had installed. He stopped dead in his tracks. "Goddamn it!"

"What?" Chaz replied.

Phelps reached forward; grabbed the lowest end of the

lock and examined it closely. "He changed the lock." Phelps said, gritting his teeth. "I need a minute."

"He's walking in right now!"

"Shit!" Phelps replied. "Park your car next to Esparza's and wait for me." Phelps regarded the yellow handles of the bolt cutters inside his bag, fully realizing, that despite his intention to use them to cut the lock, they'd do him no good at all. He zipped the bag up, snatched it in his hand and slipped out the locker room.

As soon as Phelps walked outside, he noticed the flashing headlights from Chaz's car. The signal was received and within moments, Phelps was sliding into the passenger seat. He gave his friend a stern, concerned look and closed the door with a dull thud.

"What happened, mon?"

Phelps sneered. "That son of a bitch used a high security padlock. My bolt cutters are useless."

Chaz pounded his steering wheel. "Damn it, mon."

Phelps whipped out a pair of purple surgical gloves and began sliding them on.

Chaz looked bewildered. "What da hell you doin'?"

Phelps coiled his hands and wiggled his fingers until the gloves were perfectly situated. He then leaned to his left and gripped his Glock 23 from his right-side holster and slid it free. He eyed his friend. "Plan B."

"What plan B?" Chaz pleaded.

"Is he coming?" Phelps asked.

Chaz whipped his head from side to side. "Dere's no plan B!"

Phelps loaded a round into the chamber.

"Oh, shit mon! Let's just get da hell out of here."

Phelps leaned in and knocked his fist on the dash. "Don't even think about it, brother. We're too close to let this slip away." He snapped his fingers twice, close to his astonished face. "You with me?"

Chaz curled his upper lip against his teeth and glared at his partner. "Goddam it, bruddah!" Chaz scanned the scene out his side window. He drew a breath. "Here he comes." He glanced at Phelps uneasily. "Now what?"

"He's going to take me for a little spin. We'll follow you. Take us down to that rock quarry off of 71, somewhere secluded."

They spied Esparza heading toward his car with the bag of money. He stopped before the rear end, popped the trunk, and dropped the bag inside.

Phelps watched him through the side view mirror. He waited until Esparza had slammed the trunk shut to make his move. When Esparza moved around his car to the driver's door and tugged on the handle, Phelps exited the car and was on him in an instant, jamming the nose of his sidearm into Esparza's ribs. "You just hold on right there, hot rod!"

Chaz held his weapon in his lap, listening intently to what was being said through his earbuds, waiting anxiously for his moment. When Esparza moved his hand toward his hip, Phelps pressed his gun harder. "Don't even think about it, Sunshine. Put your hands where I can see 'em!"

Chaz leaned left and right inside the car, trying to see what was going on, but his vantage point was obscured.

Esparza raised his hands slightly as Phelps leaned in and disarmed him.

"We'll open our doors together. Nice and easy..."

They opened the left-side doors and slid inside simultaneously, Esparza tucked himself in behind the wheel and Phelps plopped down into the large back seat. They closed the doors in unison. Phelps examined the car and pointed the gun at him. "Keep your hands on the wheel where I can see them." He enjoyed the spacious leg room. "We're gonna take this cool ride of yours for a little spin."

Esparza turned down the left corner of his mouth in disgust. He started the car and cleared his throat. "Where we goin'?"

Phelps motioned forward with a quick nudge of his gun. "See that car?"

Esparza turned. "Yeah."

"Follow it!"

"Where's he going?"

"It's a surprise!"

Esparza looked into the rear-view mirror and said, confidently, "I was with someone. He'll be following."

"Bullshit," Phelps challenged. "Pasetta's got his money. He's long gone."

Esparza's voice squealed, "You gonna kill me?"

Phelps winced. "I don't give a shit about you."

Esparza offered a hand as he pulled it off the wheel. "Just take it and let me go."

"Did you do your laundry?"

"It's clean, yeah."

Twenty minutes later, the wheels from the two cars churned up a cloud of dust as they turned off the pavement onto the dirt and gravel road leading deeper into the rock quarry. They rounded an immense mound of limestone gravel, four cars high, and continued past a grater and a row of three dump trucks parked evenly in a line along the makeshift lane that wound up and around the hillside.

"Pull in by those two big rigs."

Esparza did as he was told, came to a complete stop and put the car in 'Park.'

"Turn off the engine."

The only audible sound in the car once Esparza turned off the engine was his own heavy breathing.

"Good boy, now take out the keys, and drop them on the passenger-side floorboard."

The keys plunked down onto the rubber mat as Chaz exited his car and walked up to the rear of their car. Chaz rapped on the trunk twice with his knuckles.

Esparza huffed, reached down and hit the release lever. The trunk sprang open. Chaz saw that Phelps was in the back seat. He withdrew his weapon and pointed it at Esparza. Phelps exited the side door and jumped into the front passenger side next to Esparza. Chaz grabbed the bag, slammed the trunk closed and took it back to his own car. Once inside, he placed it on his lap and drove his car a short distance until the red glowing tail lights were all that could be seen to the naked eye.

Chaz unzipped the bag and inspected the bundled 100-dollar bills. He spoke into the mic and grinned. "Cool, mon. It's all here." He fumbled around inside for a few seconds and continued. "No ink." I'll pull up front and keep an eye out."

Phelps watched in the rear-view mirror until the brake lights went out and darkness sat heavily over the area once again.

"See you in a few. Nice work Danny."

Phelps eyes narrowed and he turned slowly toward his prey. They locked eyes.

"You're going to kill me, aren't you?"

Lacking all empathy or compassion, Phelps nodded. "I am."

Esparza's eyes welled up. He held both open palms toward Phelps and pleaded, "Please, Mister. Let me go. I don't even know who you are." His lower lip began to tremble and he began to sob. He shook his head from side to side. "Please? I have a family."

Phelps blinked thrice and raised his gun, pointing it directly at the younger man's head who gazed at him with terror-stricken eyes. "No, you have no family."

In a blinding flash, Esparza whipped his hand across and struck Phelps' shooting arm, knocking the gun out of his hands. It clanked against the closed window and fell down onto the floor. Phelps was stunned at the unlikely turn of events. Then, Esparza drew a knife from the concealed horizontal sheath attached to the left side of his seat. He wrapped it tightly in his right hand, and sent it towards Phelps in a tight curving arc. Relying on his training and experience, Phelps reflexively shot his own hand forward and struck Esparza's radial nerve with enough force to cause him to lose his grip. He then sent in his elbow to strike Esparza clean across the jaw. He turned the blade on Esparza who tried vainly to resist, but could do nothing to stay the fate the seasoned detective had in store for him. The look of horror quickly turned to shock as Phelps slid the blade slowly into Esparza's temple and twisted it. The fatal blow sounded like the cracking of a lobster shell and it forced Esparza into the cold void of death's embrace.

"Sleep, bad man," Phelps said, as he yanked the blade free and retrieved his gun. "Sleep."

As the man's head slumped over against the glass of the driver's side window, Phelps got out of the car, closed the door and walked away toward the red brake lights of the not too distant car.

"One less perp in the world. Justice is served."

Chapter 10

DETECTIVE PHELPS HELD his forehead in his left hand and rubbed his temples with his fingers. He stared down at his feet and the room began to spin. He stumbled toward the bar and passed the laundered half-million dollars littering the entire surface of his pool table as if the haul meant absolutely nothing to him at all. He snatched a glass decanter and, because of his inebriation, he struggled to center the spout directly over his cocktail glass. When he poured, he managed to spill most of the liquor over the left side of the glass. For the first time in his life, he knew that even liquor couldn't alleviate the guilt and the shame of what he had done. Not this night. Instead, the quarter-full glass sat there, its beckoning call falling on deaf ears. He didn't notice that the white cocktail napkin the glass was resting on had been saturated enough so that the liquor ran off the edge of the bar and started to drip onto the mahogany wooden floor. The heavy splashing sounds it made sent him into a thick haze where he was forced to recall the dripping sound of the falling drops of blood striking the driver's side door once he'd stabbed Esparza in the head. The flashback of Esparza's death expression replayed over and over in his mind and he could do nothing to shake the terrible memory.

Phelps leaned back against the pool table and let out an exasperated sigh. Tears streamed down his face. He cringed. He raised his quivering palms to eye level, realizing the scope and the magnitude of what he had done and sobbed until he finally sank his head in his hands. His strained breathing and the sounds of his crying escaping through his loosely-knit fingers were the only sounds to be heard in the room.

After a moment of further inner-reflection, he dropped his hands and stared into the glass at the one and only thing that could steal him away from the sickeningly haunting feeling growing in his core. Struggling to remain standing, he raised the glass to his open mouth and poured the minute amount of liquor down his throat. It stung, almost as severely as the sting of knowingly and willingly committing the most heinous sin of them all. Phelps set the glass down and turned around to face the pool table. He propped his arms down upon it to support himself while he regarded the piles of cash lying before him. He sneered at the sheer lunacy of it all. Money, greed, power. '*None of it is worth a dam*n,' he knew. He thought about the pain his actions would cause his parents and his sister if they ever found out about what he had done. 'What would Alex think of me?' he thought. Phelps swiped his open hands across the length of the pool table, scattering the bills everywhere. He looked up and stared into the Budweiser mirror hanging on the wall. Instead of seeing the image he had been presenting to the world all of the years he had been posing as a public servant, he saw a dark, aged, mottled, ghastly version of himself, the end result of all of the wrong doing, all the bad choices he had made—the monster he had become.

Then his eyes shifted toward the coffee table. There, his gun rested securely inside its leather holster. It was the righteous sleeve which held the justice-bringing instrument, a tool to be used only in self-defense and only as a last resort to save the lives of innocent civilians. It was a lie back then and it was lie now.

He stared at it long and hard for a solid minute and a half

before finally stumbling over toward the coffee table it was resting on. He knew that it alone could spare him from further torment, from a life he finally admitted to himself that had become one filled with emptiness and pain. He plopped down onto the sofa, clutched the holster and traced his index finger over the soft leather. It felt good in his hand, but he knew he was no longer a good man, not in the least. He slid the gun free. The metal felt cold. He checked the full magazine. 'Maybe it's time,' he thought to himself as he exhaled forcefully.

Instead, he turned to regard the adjacent wall which was host to a collection of his proudest achievements, awards and accolades, bound securely inside the sturdy, walnut case his proud father had made for him. First, he regarded the Medal of Valor he had received. He felt a warmth inside and nodded confidently because he knew that at that time in his early career, he was indeed a badass cop and his intentions were honorable. When he thought about his past, he realized he had everything going for him at that time. His life was blossoming and most importantly, he had a beautiful, dedicated and supportive fiancé standing proudly by his side.

Then he regarded his greatest achievement of them all—the Medal of Honor. He smiled broadly.

He became mesmerized with the ticking sounds that came from his gold Rolex watch sitting on the coffee table. With each tick, the memorable moments of his earlier career meandered slowly down a twisted path which grew much darker, convoluted and more perilous as the years had progressed.

He had become obsessed with the power, presumed authority, and control that came with the badge and the many other symbols of power and fear. Eventually, the allure of personal gain overshadowed them all. Collectively, they took hold of him and spread like a pervasive cancer until they dictated his every action and reaction. In his mind, he knew that he had rapidly descended from esteemed public service to downright criminality. At that point, he knew full well that he didn't serve or protect those whom he had sworn to. Rather, he placed the well-being and the lives of his fellow officers over and above the many innocent civilians he'd continually abused. The police organization he had once been proud to work for morphed into a fraternal order whose group ideology was to look away when one of its own officers overstepped their bounds or when they violated the law. These days, it was hardly ever about true public service unless there was a camera nearby. It had all devolved into a sick game. A farce. Every last part of it, he knew. The pride he had felt moments earlier turned to revulsion and remorse. And he wept from the cellars of his very soul.

Phelps descended into a feeling of dread and despair, a deep, black pit, from which, this time he knew, there would be no escape. Eventually, he came to realize, he would be judged for his crimes and his sins, of that he was certain. He propped his elbow up on his thigh and his head sank into his open palm. He knew, it would be the last warm comfort he would ever feel. For the world's sake, the world needed to be rid of him, forever.

After a few minutes, Phelps peered through his parted fingers. He saw the framed photographs of the police commissioner shaking his hand while he accepted the Rookie of the Year Award, photos taken with the Mayor of Austin and the Chief of Police while he was in full uniform with the many medals they had also earned, pinned securely to their own chests.

Phelps looked back down into his lap and the weapon he held in his hands. 'Time to end this charade,' he huffed. His entire life began flashing before his eyes. Vivid images of his brief happy early childhood were overcome by dark and foreboding scenes of despair and emptiness. His abuse of power began to suffocate him. How many lives had he ruined simply because his own life had been ruined? How many young people did he set up by pulling them over illegally; by planting evidence and by falsifying statements to hide his own missteps in an effort to enrich himself? Phelps' mind became a blur. He was no better than the lowest forms of scum he had interacted with all these years. 'I don't deserve... to go on... ' he thought.

His finger coiled around the trigger. He'd wait, he thought, just a bit longer. He sniffled and squeezed his eyes shut. All he could do... was... breathe.

Slowly, but surely, Phelps' body and mind became more and more numb. The alcohol and the overwhelming sadness forced him to succumb to the stillness of sleep. As he fell back on the couch, a silent dream took him away into a series of striking images which came within an instant and took his consciousness away like a thief in the night.

* * *

The golden rays of the sun rose abruptly above the horizon... A new beginning. A single white dove rode the warm, gentle breeze above him... A divine messenger. His younger self withdrew a Samurai sword from its sheath... A symbol of courage. Michelangelo's painting, 'The Creation of Adam... ' divine light reaching out to the darkness, the soul reaching out to Phelps, the galactic family reaching out toward the earth, shimmering in the sun's brilliance. His mother Lisa silently screaming, "No! No," as she cradled Alex in her arms while he drew his final breath... Alex reaching for him, crying, "Help me, Danny..." An American bald eagle soaring high in the sky with its wings fully spread... Freedom and inspiration to shape his life and become whatever he so desired. Danny embracing his mother while the coroner zipped shut the body bag of his dead brother... A police officer writing the report... The many symbols of power and prestige on the officer's body, the badge, the gun, the uniform, the dangling nightstick, and finally, the handcuffs... A butterfly emerging from its cocoon, fluttering away on a warm wind's current... Humanity emerging from the old paradigm to become a beautiful new evolving species.

As Phelps slept, slumped over on the sofa, the automatic timer on the lamp beside him snapped the lights off. Phelps' eyes flashed open, though they weren't his physical eyes at all. After a brief moment of disorientation, Phelps' shimmering astral body rose up out of his unconscious physical body. This light body was made of a finer substance altogether, intangible and glowing from within. As he grew more accustomed to his current state of being, he saw that the only physical light source in the room was the red hue cast from the nearby digital alarm clock sitting beside the couch on the night stand. It created an even crimson line down his physical body's cheek until the minute symbol changed. When he looked over, he saw that the time was 2:22am.

He noticed that in his current form, he felt none of the sedating effects of the alcohol or the accompanying exhaustion that his physical body would have been experiencing. In fact, he was completely and fully energized in a way that far surpassed his youth.. He moved as silently and as easily as a gentle breeze, right off the couch until he was standing, remarkably enough, beside his very own passed-out body lying there motionless before his ever-astonished eyes. He paused to let it all register in his psyche. Phelps tilted his head down and noticed a searing white illumination around his hands and arms as he brought them up before him to examine further. They were not solid appendages at all. Though they looked and appeared to be real, they were merely energetic overlays where his arms and hands *should have been.* He immediately began to question whether or not he had 'died.' When he examined the rest of his body, he noticed that his entire torso was glowing in the same beautiful way. His light body had fully moved out and away from the only body he had ever known. Energized and more aware and awake than he could ever remember, Phelps turned and smiled. Then he felt strange tingling sensation emanating from within and before he knew it, he dematerialized out of the room completely.

Instantly he found himself slowly walking through a forest dark and damp, heavy with the smell of top soil and musk. He could see clearly, yet he knew he had no physical eyes. He could hear the chirping sounds of the insects, though he understood he had no physical ears with which to hear them. Finally, as he looked around, enthralled at the prospect, he realized that he had no physical brain with which to discern what exactly he was seeing, smelling and hearing. He was a disembodied spirit lurking in the Primordial Abyss.

A large moon hung on the horizon and a thick blanket of clouds masked most of the soft off-white glow it provided. Phelps cautiously wandered through the forest like a babe through the woods. As he progressed, he instinctively moved his hands before him in an attempt to brush away the tree branches that hindered his passing, yet he quickly realized that there was no need, for his immaterial form simply passed right through them. He felt minuscule sparks as he moved through the leaves, tiny packets of living energy interacting with his own light body, captivating him in this other-worldly experience he was having.

Phelps came to an abrupt halt, digging the toe of his spectral foot into the ground and straight through some exposed roots. He cocked an ear, or at least he focused his attention where his physical ears would have been if he were a solid body. He scanned his surroundings. A preternatural sparkle saturated the leaves swaying above him and he felt a life-sustaining energy everywhere nearby.

He narrowed his focus when he heard some form of moaning. '*Where was it coming from?*' he wondered. Then he zeroed in toward the thick wooded expanse before him. He felt tingles in the top of his scalp when he heard the telltale sounds of deep, guttural chanting close by. His instinctive impulses prodded him into action. But what could he do if something was required of him when he was nothing more than a phantom?

As astonishing at it was, Phelps found himself gliding toward the direction he was focusing on by simply *desiring* to move there. As he passed further into the woods, he came to a clearing. There before him, laced in ivy and green moss lay the cracked ruins of a dilapidated stone altar. Fallen leaves rushed by and through his translucent legs. He noticed how there was very little, if any, discernible energy left in them and when Phelps gazed downward, he realized he was standing on some sort of ancient stone dais. He knelt low and traced his spectral fingers along the many blackened etchings, symbols he could not recognize and a language with which he was unfamiliar.

Yet, somehow, he knew this place.

A long, growing, whispering breeze wound its way through the trees which caused Phelps to turn sharply, this way and that until he finally gazed up into the majestic, starlit sky. There, 10,000 suns twinkled in the black shroud blanketing the sky.

Phelps felt an instant connection as if he were somehow intertwined with them all on a level far beyond his understanding. Without warning, a dissociative energy pattern rose up from the ground beneath him and oscillated in pulsating waves throughout the very core of his being. He was surrounded by a brilliant column of golden light.

When the remarkable interaction was finally over, the moon was partly obscured over the horizon and the birds were beginning to sing. Their combined calls created the most beautiful chorus he had ever heard. It was then that he was gently guided to glance down toward the base of the altar. He leaned over gradually and discerned the many drops of dried blood splattered about. They were partially obscured by a series of decaying leaves and twigs. He focused intently on the blood-stained rocks and a supernatural wind carried the debris off in its wake. He then heard the sound of footsteps crunching the dried-out leaves nearby as the feet made a circuit around him. When he peered into the grass, he spied the worn, leather, child-sized shoe, speckled with blood.

* * *

Danny Phelps groaned in his bed, rolled over onto his side and forced his eyes open. He didn't recall ever getting up from the sofa and crawling into bed. 'Add that to the continuing stack of crazy shit happening to me,' he thought. He was also thankful that he hadn't blown his brains out all over the living room. He then sat up on the edge and rubbed his eyes and massaged his scalp. Finally, he rose to his feet before the standing mirror. Hung over and hazy-eyed, he had to do a double-take when he glanced at his reflection. "What the..." Phelps gawked at his perfectly-toned body and ran his hands over his smooth, chiseled abdomen. Somehow, overnight, in fact, his body had regained the youthful perfection he had enjoyed in his early twenties, and more. He shook his head in disbelief. Then he caught the foreign object sitting perilously close to the edge of his tall dresser. He reached a trembling hand out and picked up the young girl's blood-stained shoe. "But... this was just... a dream."

Chapter 11

TERRA WRAPPED HER knuckles around the top of Phelps' hand and in between his fingers. She gave him a wild-eyed look, turned sharply toward the private lounge and tugged on him forcefully. Phelps acquiesced, without looking around him to figure out what in the world was spooking the beautiful, voluptuous dancer. She led Phelps by the hand straight past the gargantuan black bouncer who winced briefly, he too trying to discern what the rush to the safety of the back room was all about. Nervously, Terra cupped a tender hand on the bouncer's shoulder and panted, as she eyed the bar, "Don't let that guy in!"

The bouncer opened the door for them and Terra tugged Phelps inside.

"Damn, Terra," he said. "What's going on?"

She led him to a L-shaped booth and they sat down next to each other.

"Listen, something very strange is going on!"

Phelps laughed. "You have no idea..."

Terra turned to face the tinted window and Phelps followed suit. They could see the shape of an overweight man making his way hurriedly toward the door. Then the strong, powerful arm of the bouncer moved out to block his entry. Terra breathed a sigh of relief when she saw the bouncer's head move from side to side, forcing the man to back off a step.

"That guy totally freaks me out!"

Phelps leaned in and asked, "Who is he?"

Terra exhaled forcefully and shook violently like a dog expelling a pesky flea with a quick series of shakes. "He was in here last Sunday. We have half-off table dances on Sundays. He apparently didn't know that. I sure the hell wasn't going to tell him. I say, 'fuck him.' Let the buyer beware."

Phelps turned to watch the men argue. "Oh, he's aware, alright." He shook his head. The guy was after his lost money. "Damn, Terra. Why do you do this?"

Terra scowled. "Do what?"

"This. Hanging all over big, fat, sweaty old men." He grimaced. "How do you do it?"

Terra huffed. "It's not so bad. I guess you can get used to anything after a while." She smirked. "Besides," she continued, "the money's great. My house is paid for. So is my Porsche. I have some really good investments, too." She signaled a nearby waitress to bring them drinks. She leaned back, confidently. "I plan to retire by the time I'm 35."

Phelps raised a brow. He'd been working his ass off on the streets, sticking his neck out for over 20 years and she'd been kissing the necks of old perverts for far less time than that, and...

"Once, I retire, I'm going to spend the rest of my life doing whatever I want."

"Nice plan," Phelps replied, snidely. "If... you don't lose yourself in the process..."

"Look who's talking!" Terra countered. "How do you do what *you* do?"

Phelps nodded. "Point taken. I suppose when we're knee deep in it, we do get used to it after a while." He squeezed Terra's hands. "Whatever *it* turns out to be." He smiled broadly. "I guess we're just a couple of junkies addicted to our chosen line of work."

"Yeah, I guess so," Terra smiled. "Besides," she continued... she rolled her eyes as if she were viewing something inside her mind... "Some really cute guys come in here. They really balance out the old-creep factor, if you know what I mean." She sighed in relief. "And... they can be lots of fun."

Phelps tossed his head toward the tinted window.

Terra looked, "What now?"

"Looks like Romeo is being escorted out of here."

Seconds later, the cocktail waitress moved in between them with a tray of drinks and set them down on the cocktail table. Terra winked at her and Phelps followed suit.

"Terra, can I ask you a personal question?"

Terra pondered for a moment and finally acquiesced.

"You ever get involved with your customers?" Phelps asked quizzically.

Terra lurched back. "Romantically?" she scoffed. "Never! This job is strictly business. I let them think of me as the woman of their dreams." She sipped her drink. "In the end, I send them home to their wives or girlfriends without a dime they came in with, and they always... come back." Terra smiled. She paused briefly and finally spurted out, "How about you? Do you ever get involved with your... customers?"

Phelps chuckled. He was more amused than shocked. The term 'customer' really hit a nerve. "No." He shook his head and pursed his lips. "There's plenty of opportunity though, that's for sure." He looked around, fighting his embarrassment. "Plenty of opportunity." The sound system changed the ambiance to a romantic mood instantly. "I don't know, Terra. I just don't see myself in a relationship." They glanced at each other. Moments of an unusually comfortable silence followed.

She looked deeply into his eyes. "Danny?" Terra asked.

"Yeah?"

She looked at him coyly. "Can I... ask *you* a personal question?"

Phelps took a sip of his drink and Terra scooted closer toward him without him noticing.

"Sure," he said confidently.

"Have *you* ever been in love?"

Phelps nodded. "Sure." He smiled briefly.

Terra began to glow. "Don't you think... being in love is the most wonderful thing in the world?" She coyly scooted even closer so that her thigh was pressing against his. Phelps suddenly noticed her right next to him. He was a bit shocked at first and then felt comforted by her closeness and openness. When Terra slowly coiled a delicate hand around the back of his neck, weaving her fingers into his thick black hair, he began to open up to her and share the most intimate and blissfully-romantic experience he ever had, 18 years earlier...

* * *

The sun was hot and blaring, streaming down over the pristine beaches of Sapphire Beach Resort in St. Thomas, U.S. Virgin Islands. Iguanas sunned themselves, perched high above the ground in the palm trees swaying in the gentle Caribbean breezes. A dozen ducks waddled about the shore and from high above, a pelican dove into the ocean in search of its next meal. The sun's reflection glittered over the refulgent teal-colored ocean's surface.

As she lay in the lounge chair, Kristi Phelps stretched her long legs and pointed her red-painted toenails toward the ocean. She put her hand up to her brow, turned toward Phelps and smiled broadly. "Mrs. Phelps sure does have a nice ring to it."

Danny Phelps spun around off his lounge chair and knelt in sand as soft as powdered sugar. Phelps gently took her hand and brought it up to his lips. He kissed her fingertips and her wedding ring, then he proceeded up the inside of her palm and wrist. "My love," he beamed. You are so exquisite in this scenery."

Kristi arched her back to accentuate her curves and she tossed her hair over the back of the chair. "It's so beautiful here, Danny. It truly is... paradise." Her eyes sparkled and Phelps leaned and kissed her softly on the lips.

"I want to bring more beauty into your life!" He glanced at the ocean and the bright pastel sails on a nearby catamaran. He pointed toward the cove off the furthermost edge of the shore. "Imagine our dream house on the seashore, surrounded by liquid glass." He turned to face her. His eyes were practically glowing. "Amazing sunsets..." He kissed her again. "Making love in our very own private paradise. Our new life together..."

Kristi stroked the side of his face and gazed deeply into his eyes. "I just might be the luckiest girl in the world." Then she drifted back to the truth of the matter. "If only you could get more free time..."

Phelps laughed. She was right. "My work definitely is time-consuming."

A breeze caught strands of Kristi's hair which she brushed aside and tucked behind her ear. "But look how fast you made detective already." Phelps nodded. "Even before you made Rookie of the Year and the Medal of Honor."

"And I do love it. I really have found my passion."

"You're brilliant at what you do." Kristi grinned. "Quite phenomenal, actually."

Phelps leaned in and placed his elbow on her chair's armrest and smiled tenderly at her. "It really isn't that tough, sweetie." He wrapped an arm around her, so that they could look at the water together. He ran a hand over her slender hip.

"That's because you've found your gift," Kristi said. She caressed his muscular arm and kissed his shoulder.

"I know, sweetie... those Anderson murders... it was as if I already knew who did it."

She nodded and looked into his eyes. "Sweetheart, you were born to do precisely what you do."

"Just like you were born to be by my side," he replied, warmly and affectionately. "You were born to be my sweetheart, baby!"

"I love you so much, Danny." She kissed him passionately.

"I love me, too, Kristi," he interjected.

Playfully, she slapped his arm.

"I'd love you more if you..."

Phelps knew what she was after, so he jumped up and grinned at her. "You'd love me more if I went and got us some cocktails." He smiled. He was always all too eager to please.

Kristi pursed her lips. "Mai Tai, please."

Phelps spun around and pulled on his Tommy Bahama shirt which he intentionally left unbuttoned. Kristi admired his abdomen briefly. She kissed her index finger, reached out and gently traced an even line down from the center of his abdomen to his navel as he slid his Ray Bans in place, raised his eyebrows and looked at Kristi over the rim of his sunglasses. "Kristi, I've never been so happy. You're the light of my life, Sweetheart."

Kristi looked up at him and extended her hand. "I will always love you."

Phelps beamed at her. Then he took her hand once more and kissed it. He could have held it forever, but she withdrew. "I'll be back before you know it." Phelps spun around and took off toward the bar.

As he approached the exposed roots of the Sea grape

trees, he noticed a pretty elderly blond woman holding up a glittering sapphire blue necklace extended horizontally with an end in each of her fingers. "Have you seen these?"

The sparkles captivated him enough to stop to regard her. "Kristi would love that!"

The woman beamed. "They're magnetic bracelets." She wound it around her wrist and each small black magnetic stone clinked together as if by magic. "They can be bracelets..." She unwound it easily and wrapped it around her neck. "Necklaces..." Finally, she would it up through her hair. "Even as hair ties."

Phelps simply loved the idea. He imagined all the ways Kristi would wear that beautiful piece of jewelry and how beautiful she would look doing so. "How much is it?"

"Twenty dollars."

Phelps scoffed. "Sold!" He fished out a folded twenty from his shorts pocket and handed it to the kind woman who handed him his new gift for Kristi. They smiled at one another briefly.

A second later, he was off toward the tiki-style hut sat nestled between two of the main resort buildings. When Phelps arrived, he walked right up to the bar and signaled the bartender. "Two Mai Tai's, please." The frozen rum drinks were out of this world. Kristi already had one not too much earlier, and even one could send your head spinning. They were stronger than they looked, but nothing was as refreshing under the Caribbean sun.

The middle-aged African woman smiled briefly, more out of reflex than expressing any genuine kindness toward him. Through the years, Phelps had developed a keen sense when it came to reading people. He surmised that the woman had likely been serving vacationers for far too many years and that Phelps was just another customer to quickly satisfy and send on his way. She was a far cry from the kind lady he'd just met on the beach.

He then turned and looked to his right side and saw an elderly couple standing there quietly holding hands. He noticed the small, wizened woman was smiling brightly up at him. He could not mistake her genuine kindness, so he nodded at her and gave her a curt smile. He was somewhat shocked that she called out to him in such a direct manner. "You look like you just married the woman of your dreams, young man."

Phelps felt slightly embarrassed, but pride overtook him. "I did," he boomed. He then lowered his voice and leaned toward her. "It's that obvious?"

The woman smiled brightly. "I know that look." She glanced lovingly at her husband and ran her weathered fingers over his arthritic hand.

The man cupped his free hand over hers and turned to regard Phelps. He said, "I gave my wife that same look, son."

"He hasn't lost it, since," she added. She radiated an inner warmth which Phelps found quite comforting.

"How long have you been married?" Phelps asked them.

"Sixty-four years," the man replied.

Phelps cocked his head. "Congratulations." Phelps turned his head briefly to see how his drinks were progressing. When the blender began churning the ice cubes, he asked, "What's your secret?"

The other bartender slid the elderly man his tab. He turned away and began tending to it. The woman stared at Phelps with big, bright, glassy eyes. She touched Phelps' hand and said, "Love... is the key, young man." She was practically glowing, basking in what was sure to be a love that had never wavered and could never wane. "Love has always been the key."

Phelps felt a pressure in his chest. The woman held her

open palm out before his chest and even though she was not close to touching him, he felt an intense warmth on his flesh. Her message continued. "It's the gateway to your soul, to your true multi-dimensional self. Always remember that."

When her husband had finished, he signaled that he was ready to escort her to the small group of round café tables sitting nearby in the sand.

Phelps was nearly paralyzed when he pondered the magnitude of the chain of events which led up to that very moment and the powerful encounter he had just had. The man and woman walked away, hand in hand, and the woman turned back again smiling as brightly as ever. She turned back toward the table and her husband wrapped his arm around the small of her back and held her slender waist as he helped her into her seat.

When Phelps turned back around toward the bar, he saw the two tall plastic hurricane cups full of an icy mixture of Cruzan rum, Bacardi Orange rum, Pineapple Curacao liqueur, Grand Marnier liqueur, and a floater of Bacardi 151. He began to salivate. He knew how very pleased the love of his life would be when he returned to her, carrying her favorite refreshing treat. He handed the bartender his credit card and the woman smiled. She may not have been very enthusiastic about taking his order, but she certainly showed a genuine interest in getting paid for her labor. That part, Phelps knew, she enjoyed immensely. Phelps grinned at her. The corners of her mouth turned up in a smile. She knew it as well as he did.

Phelps made his way around the volleyball net and into the deeper sand toward the shore. It was softer and easier on the feet and the scenery was beyond breathtaking.

When Phelps came closer to their lounge chairs, he noticed, much to his surprise, that Kristi's chair was vacant. Her turquoise sarong was draped over the uppermost edge and her sandals were laying perfectly aligned at the foot of the chair. He wrinkled his brow. Then, like the sound of breaking glass, a piercing scream from the waterline forced Phelps and just about everyone else nearby to look toward the ocean. Phelps knew it couldn't possibly be anything he had to be concerned with, but something in his heart completely sank into the deepest recesses of despair. He saw a small group of people gathering around two forms, slumped over on the sand. Small waves lapped against their limp bodies, rocking them ever so slightly... and one of them looked like... his new bride.

Phelps flicked open his slick, wet hands and the cups hadn't even fallen into the sand before he was already sprinting toward the water's edge as fast as his powerful legs could carry him. Every muscle in his body was rapidly firing and sharp needles twanged in his thighs as his feet kicked up sand with every forceful lunge forward. As he ran closer, he could unravel the horror unfolding before him.

When he closed in, he leapt over a boogie board and planted both feet into the sand. Anguish consumed him as he saw Kristi lying motionless on her back. Her beautiful hair and face were sparsely blotched with wet sand. "Kristi!"

Just as many onlookers were gathering around, Phelps drove his knees into the sand and lowered his ear to Kristi's lips to listen for signs of breathing. Phelps whipped his head up, shocked that he had heard nothing. At the same time, the boy's mother and father rolled him gently onto his back and the man immediately began performing CPR. Phelps carefully and expediently inserted his finger into Kristi's mouth to ensure her airway was unobstructed and he was stunned to feel that her entire esophagus was clear. He quickly rolled her onto her side and pressed upon her abdomen in an attempt to expel any water that might have found its way into her lungs. He knew time was of the essence if she had any chance at all to survive. He panted and cried out in desperation.

Dribbles of sand moved out past her lips. When Phelps examined her chest, and when he saw neither rise, nor fall, he pressed against her abdomen again. Water and more sand spurted from her lips, a sign he hoped that she could still be saved. Yet, much to his dismay and to those gathering around, she remained unmoving and unresponsive.

He began thumping against her chest with his palms. Panicking now, his wild eyes told bystanders that the situation was dire. He pinched her nose and forced open her jaw by pressing down on her chin. A tear rolled down his face as he drew an ominous breath, rushed down and pressed his lips against hers and forced the air into her mouth, throat, and lungs. He heard the sounds of coughing and the spewing up of water, but he knew that it was not Kristi who was recovering, but the young boy beside her instead. He pulled away from his beloved's mouth and surveyed the scene, hoping for a sign, for something... anything that would give him the slightest glimmer of hope.

"Come on, Kristi!" he panted, wrapping the knuckles of both hands together and pressing continuously against her chest. "Come on..."

The mother wept and moaned as she held and rocked her child in her arms. Phelps looked up and around him at the gathering of people encircling them, some merely standing there with shocked faces, while others stood with their hands across their mouths. Phelps felt the elderly man's hand on his shoulder. When he looked up, he was shaking his head. Phelps laid his hands upon Kristi's chest. She was already growing cold. Her lips were turning purple and her skin was growing pale.

Waves of torment crashed over him just like, he presumed the ocean's waves took her life.

His lower lip was trembling and tears poured out of his eyes. He locked eyes with the crying mother as she rocked her resuscitated son back and forth, sobbing. Phelps dug his hands and arms under his wife and held her tightly against himself. He wept and the tears splattered onto her beautiful face and into her thick, lush eyelids which he knew would never again open. The weight of her lifeless body slumped down into the sand as her loose arm and head slid backwards into his final embrace.

As tears rolled down his distraught face, Phelps looked up to regard the mother who gave him a brief, grief-stricken expression. Phelps looked around, trying to figure out what in world had happened. He studied the waterline and saw that a terrible rip current had formed and had been sucking water away from the shore. When he realized that Kristi had likely been caught in it, he looked back at the mother and child. Their eyes told him everything he needed to know. Kristi had saved the boy's life at the expense of her own.

When he looked beside him, the sun reflected off of the beautiful sapphire-colored magnetic bracelet he had purchased for his wife earlier as it lay in the sand. He realized it must have fallen out during the excitement when he struggled to revive her.

Phelps grabbed the bracelet and closed his eyes. The sound of crashing waves overcame him. The dream he had been living and the vision he had for Kristi and their shared future together had been shattered in an instant, like splintering glass.

* * *

Phelps was lost in thought. Terra's fingers had frozen in place in his hair. Her powerful words echoed again in his mind like thunderous, reverberating drums, 'Don't you think that being in love is the most wonderful thing in the world?'

Phelps' face was deadpan. He looked as if he had been drained of all life force and all that remained was an empty, hollow husk. "Yeah..." he huffed. "It really is." He looked at her. "You know, Terra..." he nodded at her. A sudden glimmer shone in his eye and he narrowly succeeded in producing a smile. "When I was in love," he continued. "...for the first time, in my life, I was... happy."

Terra gazed into his eyes and touched his arm. "Oh my God, Danny. I had no idea. I am so sorry you had to go through that."

"Watch out for love, Terra. It's a double-edged sword."

Terra gasped.

He was, of course, grateful beyond words that he was able to share even those brief years with Kristi, rather than having experienced nothing at all. However, he also seriously considered how it might have been to be spared that intense feeling of prolonged loss and agony if he had never met her at all.

Phelps took a long slow sip of his drink. It was his sole comfort these days, something to dull the pain associated with a life he knew was off track. "Love," he continued through the release of a long, intense sigh, "is every bit as painful as it is wonderful." He swallowed. "Raw and bittersweet."

Terra brushed the back of her fingers against Phelps' cheek. After Phelps turned to regard her, they looked deeply into one another's eyes and Terra slowly leaned in to kiss him. Phelps didn't hesitate. He returned her kiss and Terra leaned in closer and snuggled with him.

Phelps suddenly realized he was exposing more of himself than he had intended. He peeled her arm off his shoulder and eased her away.

"I have to go." He stood abruptly and pulled a wad of cash out from his front pocket and flicked two one-hundred-dollar bills on the table before her. He turned on his heels and hurried off.

"Danny!" she called out to him.

Phelps stopped in his tracks and turned around his head without quite looking at her.

Terra ran up to him and wrapped him in her arms.

Initially, Phelps did not respond, but he turned and put his arms around her, too. They held each other for a moment. He then said, gruffly, "I'm not the man for you, Terra." He leaned back so their eyes could meet. "I'm damaged goods."

"No, Danny..."

"Terra, I'm... broken."

Phelps knew that Terra had genuine feelings for him, but those feelings were always kept in a state of checks and balances based upon where and when she would feel comfortable enough to allow them to come out and in what capacity she was operating under at that time; a professional erotic dancer, an actress, or a woman in search of love and tender expression. Terra knew she had a brief glance at the stalwart detective's soft under belly, the side he had never revealed to anybody, the wounded side, powerfully hidden beneath that impenetrable, protective shell that he always wore.

Terra's face fell toward the floor. She looked up at him again with doe eyes. "Is there another woman?"

"There is," Phelps replied.

Terra looked defeated. "Who is she?"

Phelps raised a single brow and admitted, "I don't know."

Terra lay her head on Phelps' chest and listened to his heartbeat.

Phelps stared at the hardwood floor lost in thought and within seconds, once he looked up, his consciousness was interfacing with some other multi-dimensional reality.

* * *

Phelps was suddenly standing in an unnaturally-brilliant field of swaying green grass, a shade of green unlike anything he had ever seen, seemingly alive and pulsating with an abundant, electric radiance. It was paradise on a level beyond his wildest fantasies. His nostrils flared and he raised his head to breathe deeply in the scents of fresh, fragrant flowers carried everywhere on a warm, steady, gentle, almost indiscernible breeze. He looked upward and scanned the obscured, misty horizon and caught the august majesty of a series of shimmering waterfalls rushing down the mountainside emptying into iridescent pools which dotted the velvety landscape. His eyes followed the immense flawless slopes back down toward ground level, where he noticed groups of different grazing animals which were breathtakingly beautiful and radiating a sense of unconditional love and connectedness. He began to soak up that feeling, quenching a lifelong thirst he had harbored as if he had been nothing at all throughout his earthly life, but a dry and empty sponge.

When he stared into the marble-like eyes of the creatures studying him, he knew, instinctively, that they truly loved him as well, despite all of his faults, all of his failures and mistakes. His first glimpse into what would become known as Unity Consciousness, the reality that all living things are connected to the one, all-pervasive Source of Creation, expanded and came quickly to include him as well.

Phelps was moved to tears, yet none came. It was a feeling that he had longed for all of the days of his life. The beautiful beings nearby were clearly nothing similar to those that lived on Earth. And so, he pondered, 'Where am I,' smiling as brightly as he had ever remembered. A profound sense of peace at long last filled his soul like pulsating liquid gold was flowing through his veins.

'Wherever I now find myself,' he mused, astounded at the way he had constructed that thought, a thought that consumed him with an all-pervading feeling of unadulterated bliss, 'I don't ever want to leave.'

Phelps gasped when he sensed the presence of someone he knew with every single fiber of his being. When he focused his awareness before him, he noticed that his arms were coiled around the waist of a slender, young woman. Her long, soft, sweet-smelling black hair licked his face as it slowly danced in the otherworldly, inanimate winds. Her beauty was beyond measure. When he gazed into her eyes, the colors they emitted mesmerized him, colors he could not even begin to understand or describe to himself, for there were no such colors to be found anywhere on Earth. She was utterly breathtaking, the answer to all of his fondest desires. She appeared to be someone with the aspects and traits of both an African and a Polynesian blended together perfectly. Her skin radiated health and wellness, a soft, chocolate brown flesh as aromatic as it was breath-taking. The ends of her silk sarong seemed to coil around Phelps' legs as if they too had a life of their own. Phelps knew, without ever recalling meeting the woman in his earthy life, that she was without a doubt, his eternal Soulmate.

"You!" he beamed, lost in the splendor of her eyes. "It's you!"

"Yes, my beloved," she replied. "We are together again."

Phelps closed his eyes. He knew in his core that he would never, *he could never* desire another woman on Earth as intensely as he desired her. He yearned to remain in her tender embrace for as long as he existed. No other could possibly compare.

Suddenly, as if his every thought were being thoroughly examined, Phelps felt himself being slowly but surely torn away from her by an indiscernible, invisible force. He fought with every fiber of his being to stay with her, but his immaterial feet found nothing to hold onto to maintain his intimate embrace. He felt her slender fingers being pried from his shoulders and she too fought to cling onto him. Their eyes shared a feeling of deeply disturbing, yet temporary loss. For even though they were being torn asunder, they knew they would find one another again when the time was right for their reunion.

"My love..." beckoned the woman.

Phelps could not bear to part from her. "Please," he moaned. "No..."

Whirlwinds churned between them and pushed them even further away until Phelps found himself present yet again inside the Lonestar Gentleman's Club.

* * *

Phelps lurched back and sucked in the deepest breath as if it were his last.

"What is it, Danny?" What's happening to you?"

Phelps shook his head ever so slightly. "I know her!" He turned the corners of his lips up in a warm smile. "I know her!"

Alarmed, Terra took Phelps by the forearm. "Who are you talking about?" Terra queried. He was hot to the touch. "Danny?" she pleaded. She moved back a bit, unsure. "What's happening to you?"

Phelps knew she would never understand and it would take too much time to fill her in. "I..."

"What?"

As soon as that last word left Terra's lips, Phelps felt his cell phone vibrate on his hip. He hurriedly drew it from his belt clip and checked the screen. He nodded and pressed a tender hand against Terra's cheek. "Another time, I have to go get some sleep."

Terra rolled her hands around in her lap and groaned as her friend hurried through the door.

* * *

Phelps slid off his shoes and shuffled along the cool tile floor of the kitchen. He paused momentarily before the window as he stood beside the sink, admiring the many cedar trees in his back yard. He could barely keep his eyes open. "What a week," he mumbled to himself. He turned his head and coiled his hands around a tall water glass and turned the spigot on his stainless steel Berkey water filter until the glass was three-quarters full. He took a long, slow drink of pure, refreshing water and set the glass down on the counter. His eyelids were falling and after a long exhalation, Phelps wheeled around and walked into the foyer, wound his way around the banister and started the long climb up the carpeted stairs to the second level. With each step, Phelps found himself closer and closer to unconsciousness. By the time he made it into his bedroom, he was totally spent. He peeled off all of his clothes, slid into the warm embrace of his down comforter and by the time his head hit the pillow he was out.

* * *

As he lay in bed, hours later, Phelps became aware of a faint, steady, rumbling growl which seemed to come out of nowhere and swirl around within his mind until it faded away into obscurity. With a deep sigh, Phelps once again began to drift off to sleep. A mere moment later, the sound came again, forcing him to maneuver his head under one of his pillows in an effort to block out the disturbance. When it happened a third time, he found himself no longer resting comfortably in his bed in the twilit haze of sleep, but wide-awake, fully cognizant and excitedly walking mid-stride, barefoot along the heavily-populated beach of a tropical Hawaiian paradise he had somehow found himself in. He turned his head toward the open ocean and discovered that the sounds he had been hearing earlier were the sounds of powerful, cascading waves rolling in and crashing along the shell-littered foreshore.

The sounds of cheering children, blaring lifeguard whistles and booming Beach Boys music being broadcast from the pavilion brought a beaming smile to his face. That, coupled with the energizing heat cast down from the shimmering, mid-day sun as it beat down upon him and the hot, coarse sand grinding against the bottoms of his feet and winding in-between his toes as he walked along the water's edge were the idyllic summer day sensations of his youth. As he looked down at his toes and the foamy water rolling in to consume them, he noticed the stark contrast between the hot sand and the cool ocean water.

Phelps felt the wind pick up in his hair, so he gazed skyward to admire the fronds of a dozen majestic palm trees swaying ever so slightly in the soft, gentle breeze. Then he felt the sudden chill of the cold, salt water pelt his face as a huge foam-tipped wave climbed ominously to obscure the horizon. Phelps heard the giggling cheers of the many children in the water, and the screeching and screaming of the adults as the monstrous wave came in and crashed against the shore. That was when he thought he heard his name being called out in the distance.

"Danny!"

Phelps furrowed his brow and looked around him at the many people splayed out on their blankets and beach towels. No one was looking at him, so he wondered where the call was coming from. Then he felt the presence behind him, a haunting, familiar feeling.

When he whirled around, he saw his tanned, glowing 13-year-old brother in his navy-blue swim trunks, holding a surfboard and grinning broadly at him from behind his long, wet, sandy blond bangs which hung down past his nose.

"Alex!" Phelps reached his hand out toward him as he stood there smiling at him in the distance, a connection he had sought for so many agonizing years since they had been separated for so long.

"Come on. Grab your board! Check out those barrels!"

Phelps was stunned. He looked around himself, excitedly, and found a nearby surfboard standing upright with its tail end held buried in the sand, as if it were placed there and waiting for him for precisely this moment. Without hesitation, he lunged for the board and whipped his head around to regard his brother who was now ankle deep in the surf, eagerly waving him on. Phelps smiled as Alex ran deeper into the water. Phelps wouldn't miss this chance for anything, not for the entire, wide world. Phelps yanked the board out of the sand, tucked it under his muscular arm and sprinted with all possible speed toward his brother who was now laying prone on his own board and paddling out further, giggling all the way.

Phelps closed the distance, kicking up sand and shallow water behind him until he finally plopped his board down onto the water and lunged upon it. He drove his cupped hands into the surf and paddled as powerfully as his arms could propel him so that he could close the distance as quickly as possible. He giggled himself, so help him, giggled like a child again, for the first time in decades. When he looked ahead at the building wave, and at his older brother swinging around, Phelps felt like he was 11 years old again, a time when there wasn't a care in the world for either of them. He heard Alex's familiar panting when the wave began to build as it grew closer. "Let's make this drop!"

Phelps nodded. He paddled hard, they both did and at the precise moment, they eased up upon their boards, slid forward, found their footing and stood up, both feet firmly planted and their arms splayed out at their sides. Alex laughed and touched Danny's fingertips with his own. They smiled at one another deeply.

"Here we go, Danny," Alex panted. "Are you ready?"

A powerful energy coursed through Phelps' body. "Yeah!" he shouted. The wave nudged them both forward and began to build behind and beneath them. "You bet I am!"

Alex's giggling intensified as the huge curving arc of pristine aqua-colored sea water held both Phelps brothers firmly in its grasp and sent them coursing toward the shore.

"Totally epic, dude," Alex shouted, smiling all the way.

Alex pivoted and banked so his board cut across the wave they were riding right into the narrow tunnel created by another wave crashing in on itself. He bounced and wove his way through it and Danny followed suit. Danny looked up, mesmerized when he saw the water churning around him and before he knew it, they had both shot through the gap, banked over the top of the wave and seamlessly rushed up upon the shore until finally collapsing on their boards, looking at one another and laughing in hysterics until their sides ached. Phelps was filled with joy. He thought about how much he had missed Alex's addictive, distinct laugh. Everything about him was perfect, from the three freckles on the tip of his nose to his sparkling blue eyes. He had a better, more golden tan than he ever remembered him having, too. Danny couldn't help but stare at him and smile from the centermost core of his being for several long moments as Alex simply smiled, knowingly.

"Awesome, Danny," he said, smiling brightly.

Danny grinned. "What a bomb!" He turned to check out the incoming waves. "Let's go!"

Before he knew it, they were both paddling furiously out into the cleansing, satiating water, among the thunderous waves once more, laughing and cheering and hooting and hollering like they did so many years ago.

After their last run, Danny and Alex dragged their boards in and set them down on the sand, where they collapsed in total exhaustion, panting and relishing their day of renewed friendship and brotherhood, the way Phelps knew it was meant to be.

Moments later, as Phelps looked around him at the august majesty of the tropical paradise, the sun was now a brilliant red orb hanging low on the horizon, reflecting off the ocean as it was slowly descending to bring an end to another day.

Danny caught his breath and looked around him. The beach was sparsely populated and the last stray seagulls were making their way across the sky. Danny eased his eyes toward his brother and noticed that he hadn't aged a single day. His skin was tight; his body was toned; his youthful vigor was as present as it had ever been. Phelps then looked at his own aged hand in comparison.

"Alex," he called out, softly.

His older brother looked at him as he rested his head on his own outstretched arm.

"I..."

Alex frowned.

"I thought you were... *dead*!"

Alex smiled broadly, pausing momentarily to stare into his soul.

"No, Danny!"

Phelps waited, all too eager to hear the reply, desperate, in fact, to learn more...

"I will *never* die!"

Phelps' eyes shot open and he lay on his back. He lunged forward off of his pillow and clutched his chest, letting out a long, relieved sigh. He felt his throbbing heart against his open palm for several moments. As he did so, he felt a warmth building there in what used to be a cold, empty void. Phelps smiled warmly. The love connection he and his brother had developed in their youth had been renewed during this visitation and had fully returned. He knew that Alex, in his purest form, was very much alive and well. He also knew that somehow, Alex had not only been with him since the day he left his body, but that he was integral to the bizarre chain of events now unfolding in his current experience.

Finally, at long last, he found it within him to forgive himself for all of the guilt and shame of not acting quickly enough to save him.

Phelps smiled in serene comfort.

He could now be at peace.

Chapter 12

THE FORENSICS LAB was aglow with a series of flickering monitors and flashing lights. DNA expert Jeff Straub was slowly running his finger down the screen with one hand and writing in a notepad with the other. Then he peered through the blinds and saw Detective Phelps approaching the building from the parking lot. As Phelps entered the building, Straub poked his head out the door.

"Detective," Straub shouted. "Over here!" He waved at him.

Phelps raised a hand to signal that he had heard him and walked over toward the door.

When he'd arrived, Phelps, shook his hand and said, "Thanks for your time, Jeff."

"Not a problem," he replied. "Come on in."

Eager to learn what he had discovered, he begged, "What did you find?"

Straub eased back into his chair and spun it around to face the monitor bank he had been studying moments earlier. Without turning to face him, he asked, "Well, Detective. The most pressing question is, just where did you find this shoe, anyway?"

Phelps propped himself up on the desk by firmly placing his palm on the desk. He leaned in and asked, "Is there a problem?"

Straub looked at him briefly and then studied the screen. "I wouldn't say there's... a problem."

"Well..." Phelps pressed. "That's a good thing, isn't it?"

"Normally, yes."

Phelps frowned.

"I checked the DNA from the blood on the shoe with the hair sample you provided."

Phelps frowned even more noticeably.

"They match!"

Phelps felt elated, yet he felt that tell-tale knot growing in his stomach. The ever-elusive missing-child case he had been unable to solve for what seemed like an eternity, looked like it was finally drawing nearer to a close, and he was understandably feeling a profound sense of relief about that. However, the dirty duty that awaited him was a source of discomfort he would rather do without. 'How am I going to tell her parents?' he wondered.

A moment passed as Straub eyed Phelps incredulously.

Straub said nothing.

Phelps tapped his first three fingers on the desk. "So that's it, then."

Phelps became lost in thought. The dizzying dilemma sent a series of rapid-fire images coursing through his mind. Walking up to the front door; the cacophonous doorbell clanging inside the empty home with all its children gone; the murdered girl's parents peeling back the curtains to see who had come to call; the opening door; the first knowing teardrop rolling down the grieving mother's cheek; her husband reaching out to comfort her, and all without Phelps uttering a single word.

"No," Straub interjected. "That's not it!"

Phelps snapped out of his daydream. "What do you mean?"

"Take a look!"

Phelps shot his wild eyes at the screens where Straub was pointing.

"There's more than just the girl's DNA on the shoe."

Phelps didn't find that at all unusual. "The perp's coding is on there, too." 'Big deal,' he thought to himself.

"There's another area on the shoe that contains a completely different DNA profile." He pointed to the DNA sequence on the computer-generated chart on the large projection screen on the adjacent wall. There, two split DNA sequences sat side-by-side. "Did the girl have a pet iguana or snake or something like that?"

"I don't know," Phelps replied. "Why?" Suddenly, Phelps felt a pang in his chest.

Straub fired up his red laser pointer and zeroed in on specific places in the DNA chains. "This electropherogram is the result of my analysis."

"Obviously," Phelps replied, forcing Straub's head to spin around. "Sorry," he chuckled. "I appreciate what you're doing for me." Straub again focused on the charts. "What are we looking at?"

Straub lit up the right-side DNA sequence. "Look at the similarities. The allele in these loci match, here," he said as he waved the laser pointer around like a conductor's wand. "...and here."

Phelps moved his head to one side and held it there, as if it were suddenly frozen in place. "I see it's different, but I'm... not sure what you're getting at." He huffed. "What is this?"

Straub flicked his wrist so that the laser dot shook around the specific section of the chart. "This resembles..." he said. Suddenly, time seemed to slow considerably, so that his next few syllables dragged on and were distorted enough for Phelps to feel that the words themselves, and how they were being presented to him, shook the foundations of his world. "...Reptilian DNA!"

Phelps felt like he was hit in the forehead with a curveball. He reeled back and barely caught his balance before he righted himself. Everything that had been happening to him was coming back at him at warp speed—specifically, the vision he had had about those monstrous lizard people. 'I can't tell Straub any of this, certainly not, but how can I make excuses for my obviously strange reaction,' he wondered?

When he looked down at Straub, his expression told him all he needed to know. "Are you alright, Detective?"

Phelps cleared his throat. "Reptilian DNA?"

"Yes," he replied. "Without a doubt."

"That's not helping my investigation. What difference does it make if the DNA of a harmless, pet reptile contaminated the sample?" He laughed. "We're not looking at the killer here, are we?" He laughed again.

Instead of laughing himself, Straub was deadly serious. He pointed at various sections of the DNA sample. The red laser light was dancing around the enormous screen. "Look at this here." He moved the dot downward. "Here, and..." he continued, "...here."

Phelps shook his head again. He was purposefully remaining calm. "I'm still not sure what you're getting at, Jeff. What is it we're looking at that is making you so excited?"

Straub dropped his head in his palm and then spun around and extended it to him. "This DNA has *mutated*!" He softly bashed his closed fists on the desk before the keyboard. "It just doesn't make any sense," he continued. "It doesn't appear to be typical Reptilian DNA, either!"

"What is it, then?" Phelps snapped.

Exasperated, Straub moaned, "I don't know *what* it is. I just know..."

"Explain."

"I just know *what it isn't.*"

"Meaning... ?"

"It isn't quite fully Reptile." He tapped on the computer screen. Just how did this child's shoe come into your possession, Detective?"

Phelps' shields came up quickly. He didn't like the tone of the question. It felt more like an inquisition.

"Your report doesn't indicate the crime scene or the general location in which this shoe was found."

Phelps changed subjects. "What do you mean, it isn't quite reptile? You're not giving me a lot to go on."

"I'm saying, it's like nothing I've ever seen before." Straub ran his hand though his curly brown hair. He paused, thinking, calculating.

Phelps waited.

"I can run another electropherogram..." he continued. "... Plot the results..."

Phelps shrugged.

"But I don't think anything will change," he said, losing steam.

"So," Phelps interrupted. "The only thing we can confirm at this time is that the blood on the shoe belongs to the girl."

"Not so fast, Detective. There's more."

Phelps lowered his head.

Straub punched the keyboard and brought up another split screen. "I brought up *your* DNA from the employee database. Here's what yours looks like." Phelps leaned in, curiously. "You can see the typical double-helix DNA pattern found in all humans."

Phelps pointed to the adjacent chart. "And what's this?"

Straub regarded the pattern and gave Phelps a stone-cold look. "Detective, did you compromise this evidence at all?"

Phelps crossed his arms over his chest and glared down at the scientist. "What do you mean, Jeff?"

Straub rolled his eyes. "I mean... did you follow protocol?"

The detective was always one to answer a question with a question, simply to avoid answering the question posed to him and put the other guy in the hot seat. "Is there a problem with your results?" He extended his arms to his sides and shrugged his shoulders to profess innocence. "What are you getting at?"

"Did you pick up the shoe? Sneeze on it? Cough on it? Something? Why is your DNA on this shoe?" Straub pointed toward another chart. "Look!" he continued. "This profile is consistent with your DNA on the shoe."

Phelps groaned. He studied the two charts and then jammed his finger into the screen. "But it doesn't look exactly like the DNA in this chart."

"No, Detective, it doesn't. This DNA has mutated, similar to the mutated reptilian DNA I showed you." He pointed toward the DNA sequence he was referring to. "See these alleles are consistent with yours." He directed Phelps' attention to another part of the chart. Now, look at the DNA from the shoe. Alleles 15, 17, and 19 are indicative of mutation. But they're human in nature."

"Could there have been an error in your analysis?"

"Absolutely not, Detective. I've sequenced this DNA three times with precisely the same results. There is no mistake."

"Could there be a problem with the software program?"

Straub tapped his thigh with his fist. "That's just it. The software doesn't know what it's looking at. These mutations are just a display. This DNA doesn't even show up in the global database. But for some reason, it's almost identical to yours."

"That's just great," Phelps retorted. "So, as I said, all we know is that the girl's blood is on the shoe."

Phelps walked toward the door.

"I can't say exactly *what* you know."

Phelps opened the door.

"Detective?"

Phelps turned around.

"You never answered my question earlier about the crime scene identified in your report." He narrowed his eyes. "Where did the shoe come from?"

Phelps paused and turned his head around ever so slightly, grinning. "A shoe store... where else?" Phelps grinned, shook his head and closed the door behind him.

The engine roared to life and Phelps was out onto the highway quickly. '*Reptilian DNA...* ' The images of the hulking Reptilian humanoids abusing and murdering that poor young woman haunted his vision. He thought long and hard about what he had heard a few minutes earlier. 'Was Jeff really trying to tell me that my own DNA was... *mutating*?' he pondered. He clutched the steering wheel tighter and sneered. He thought of the vision and the children he had seen in the cages and those menacing claws being raked along the metal bars. 'Reptilian DNA,' he thought to himself over and over again. Could it be that what he had been experiencing in his uncanny visions was actually real in the physical world?

Phelps cut the wheel when he saw the Highway 304 sign blur by. That's when he realized that he'd been on a deeply-rooted trek of subconscious contemplation. He checked his speedometer and was stunned to discover that he was screaming down country roads and coursing through miles of meadows and woods at over 90 miles per hour.

"That's it!" he blurted out. He cocked his head trying to make sense of what he was suddenly thinking. Phelps slammed on the brakes and whipped his head behind him. There wasn't a car to be seen. He cut the wheel, shifted into reverse, and hit the gas. The wheels churned beneath him as he backed the car onto the gravel, and before he knew it, he was in first gear flying down the access road toward the place where his vision had taken him earlier.

Phelps wound his way around and along the paved road until he came to a narrow two-track road that was seldom used and only by wildlife conservation and game warden vehicles. Since his car had such low ground clearance, he pulled to the side and decided to continue his investigation on foot.

The sun hung above the tree tops as he closed the car door and was on his way, stepping over the guardrail and down along the chain link fence to the river's edge, a river which had degraded in intensity now to be nothing more than just a trickle in the parched, cracked riverbed.

The woods grew thicker, populated mostly by cedar trees and cacti. Phelps ducked beneath a series of thick, sturdy branches and pushed aside the smaller ones blocking his way. Something was guiding him, though he knew not what.

Then, he heard the sounds of distant chanting, ahead and over the rise. Phelps stopped suddenly and cocked his ear. This was all too eerily familiar. His eyes darted from side to side until he zeroed in on where they were likely coming from. He cautiously stepped over some fallen wood and placed foot after foot on the most open ground capable of providing the most silent approach possible.

Phelps crouched low and peered through the tangle of branches before him. He slowed when he entered the tree line, picking his way carefully through the trees and low-hanging branches. He had barely moved into the thicket before he knew, instinctively, that he had found the same place in his dream where he had discovered the shoe. 'But was it a dream at all?' he contemplated.

Phelps was suddenly stricken with a palpable sense of foreboding and doom. He crept over the rise and carefully concealed himself in a cluster of bushes by lying down as flat as he could. The chanting grew louder. He peeked through the tiny branches and peered down into the low-cut valley below him. There, precisely as he had seen it in his dream, stood the makeshift stone altar. Around it, though, stood a gathering of people wearing menacing black-hooded robes. They each wore an inverted pentagram amulet in the center of their chests, each hanging via a dull silver chain.

Phelps knew this to be a seriously dangerous situation. Then, from behind the others, came a red-robed fiend, at least a full two feet taller than the others who took his position at the head of the altar. When he raised his hand, Phelps noticed him wielding a jeweled, serrated dagger and what Phelps saw next sent him plunging into the deepest depths of dread and sorrow.

There, bound to the altar, lay a convulsing, panic-stricken, blond-haired little boy, no older than the age of six. Phelps dug his fingers into the dry underbrush and down into the coarse dirt. He leaned forward like a wolf who, after a full day of stalking, had finally zeroed in on its prey. His eyes were exploding out of his sockets. His teeth were bared. Rage and adrenaline began to course throughout his entire body. Just when it couldn't get any worse, the chanting intensified and the face and hands of the red-robed man in the valley shifted and morphed into and out of human form. Green scales overlaid the smooth rosy complexion of the otherwise normal flesh. Where there once was a normal human nose, there was now a thick, leathery, green, snorting snout of something out of this world. Phelps rolled onto his back, staring at the sky above him in debilitating shock, his mouth wide open in a silent scream.

"Help!" screamed the terror-stricken boy. "Daddy, help me..." The call was silenced as like a snuffed-out candle flame.

The chanting rose and fell until it became thunderous and booming. Phelps rolled over onto his side. Fallen leaves clung to his shirt and the seat of his pants and legs. He found his way to his knees and peered down below from within the center of a dead tree. Its leaves had already fallen and littered the ground where he now stood.

Phelps noticed a strange shadow off to his left side which he responded to by shifting only his eyes. When he saw nothing, he centered them once again. The red-robed thing held a golden chalice beside the boy's chest. From the long and terrible gash in his heart came short spurts of blood which both shot directly into the vessel and dripped down the side of his scantily-clad body.

Before he could even understand what had happened, an eight-foot-tall Reptilian appeared out of a wall of black smoke behind Phelps and pounded him in the back of the head with an immense and powerful forearm. Phelps collapsed into the fallen leaves and his eyes fluttered until he finally succumbed to calming void of unconsciousness.

Chapter 13

THE DRIFTING, BATTERED sailing vessel was listing to port when yet another massive white squall swept unhindered from the North and roared toward it. Screaming, scrambling sailors gazed up in horror as the great mast above snapped in two and threatened to fall headlong into the wooden plank deck they were all standing on. This, they knew, would surely doom them all.

Phelps turned his face to fight the biting rain. Through narrowed eyes, he scowled and scanned the horizon for the faintest hope that the storm would finally let up. Phelps grimaced. There was no hope to be found. Not now, anyway. Instead, forked tongues of lightning flashed menacingly overhead and booming thunderclaps shook the skies. Unrelenting, stabbing pain shot up and down Phelps' arms and shoulders as he clung to the thick ropes tightly, in a continuous effort to right himself as the endless, crushing waves slammed into the square rigger. When he gazed down at his hands, he saw that there was nothing at all left of his palms. The flesh there was completely shredded and soaked in blood.

A wave of freezing cold water struck Phelps square in the face and swept over his entire body, sending his black hair coursing back over his scalp. A deep, relentless chill burrowed into the core of his body and settled there, seemingly for an eternity to torment him even further. His face felt like it was being stung by 1,000 tiny needles. Distorted voices nearby came from nowhere and everywhere at once. When he was sure that the wave had passed, he gasped for one chance at a deep breath.

When Phelps opened his eyes and stared ahead of him, he found that he was not on a sailing vessel at all, but in a far different, most disturbing, yet familiar place.

The shifting silhouettes of three Reptilians moved past him like shadows in the dark. He blinked several times to clear his eyes enough to see what was going on. He tried to move his arms, but quickly discovered, much to his dismay, that he was bound to a chair by ropes which were very similar, if not identical to the crimson-stained ropes he had clung to in his most recent vision, *or nightmare*, whichever the case might have been.

Another form moved directly in front of his face, scowling at him with deeply penetrating eyes. He held a metal bucket firmly in his hands. The water inside sloshed over the rim as he threatened to hit him again. Apparently, he had been at it for quite some time and Phelps' only recollection of it was the dreamscape his mind wandered to while he was being tormented, for who knows how long. And because he had been unresponsive, or simply because the man before him enjoyed it so, Phelps whipped his head to the side and held his breath as another bucket-full of ice water struck him in the ear and nose and finally rolled down his shirt into his soaked lap. Phelps sputtered and exhaled forcefully, trying his best to clear his nostrils. He wiggled his head to clear his ear. He was desperate to bring his hand up, but he was reminded all too quickly that it was securely bound and wasn't going anywhere.

When he turned his head slowly, seething with anger, he saw his interrogator, but only just barely. Beside him, much to Phelps' surprise, stood the translucent form of the stranger who had been haunting him in the guise of a homeless man; a bar back, and a sign spinner. "What the hell are you doing here?" he demanded. He sneered at him through clenched teeth. "You in on this?"

The interrogator wheeled his head over in the direction Phelps was facing, and the look of sheer confusion led Phelps to understand that the interrogators could not see or hear the strange man at all even as it gently placed its spectral hands upon Phelps' shoulders.

Powerful, soul-wrenching reverberations cascaded throughout his entire body as the stranger spoke to him. "It is time to open your eyes to the world as it is Danny. To awaken to the truth."

A man, a real man, rather a solid man, stepped in front of the ghostly visitor, not as if he were interrupting, but as if he were completely oblivious to his presence. "So, Detective," he said, fondling Phelps' gun. "It seems you have ventured into... deep and deadly, uncharted waters at the edge of the world."

That statement shook Phelps to his core. He was bound to a chair because he had witnessed something in the woods earlier that he was not meant to. The situation, he knew, was dire indeed.

"A lamb among wolves..." the man continued.

A second man pulled a purple cloth away from the tray on the nearby table off to his side. Phelps closed his eyes tightly. It was loaded with an assortment of neatly-arranged instruments of torture. He suddenly thought of the woman he had seen in his vision. The room in which he found himself now seemed to be the very same room where the woman was murdered by the Reptilians.

"What were you doing back there?" The man leaned over to set the water bucket down, but instead, held the handle securely, wheeled around, and whipped it toward Phelps' face. Phelps cringed to block as much as the impact as possible, but it collided with his ear and bounced off his head with a giant 'gong' sound. The edge of the handle had nicked his neck, close to his jugular, but was not close enough or deep enough to threaten his life.

"Why were you back there?" the man continued, tossing the bucket away to the opposite corner of the room. "In those woods." The clamor the bucket made as it struck the ceramic tile of the floor injured Phelps even further, likely because of his current mental state, Phelps surmised.

Phelps grinned and looked the man squarely in the eyes. "Oh, ya know... just takin' a hike."

"Bullshit!"

A quick backhand slap across Phelps' face accentuated the man's reply. It struck with just the right force to split his lip. Phelps could feel the warmth of his blood trickling down and collecting on the side of his mouth. The taste of iron seemed to fill Phelps with some much-needed resolve.

"Who hikes with a gun, Detective?" He flicked the safety off and regarded Phelps with a single raised brow.

Phelps spat the blood from his mouth. It landed squarely on the man's shoe, forcing his face to contort into one which exhibited seething rage.

"You never know..." Phelps said, as if he were posing a question, rather than a statement, but then it became glaringly obvious as he finished his statement. "...when you'll meet up with some sick, twisted fucks torturing innocent children!"

The clenched fist was but a blur as it swept in from the side and struck Phelps in the right eye.

The pain was intense, the kaleidoscope colors caused by the blast refracted in on one another. Phelps waited for both the discomfort and the distortions to subside. He sat there motionless, fully expecting to be struck again.

Instead, a soft humming sound filled his head and Phelps felt like he had shifted to another place, altogether. He again felt a pair of warm and reassuring hands press gently against the top of his shoulders.

Phelps knew that he and he alone could hear the reassuring voice from behind. "Your pain will heal you, Danny."

Blood dripped into Phelps' eye from the gash on his brow. He raised his chin and blinked several times, forcing it to seep out of the corner. The stinging sensation debilitated him. The other man in the room wheeled the table of torture instruments around from the side, so they were squarely in sight of Phelps' rapidly expanding and terror-stricken eyes. This maneuver caused Phelps to genuinely fear for his very life. 'Who were they?' he wondered. 'What the hell was going on inside this city?'

"What..." the man barked, sending shivers up Phelps' spine, "...did you see?"

The calm voice from the inner guide behind him eased his nerves. "Don't hold back, Danny. Tell them everything..."

Phelps swallowed hard. This was his chance to tell them, to tell his maker what had been eating away at his soul since he was but a child. "I saw the demise of millions of children who are abducted each year."

The interrogators brow furrowed.

"Leaving their parents, families, and loved ones in a state of hopelessness and anguish that they take with them when they leave this tortured world." Astonished and disgusted at the same time, Phelps saw the smug prick clapping his hands slowly.

"Bravo, Detective. You've figured it all out, haven't you?" He grinned at him from ear to ear like the sick, sadistic, evil prick that Phelps knew him to be. "What else?" he demanded.

"Sex slaves…" Phelps challenged.

The man's eyes lit up.

"…to the elite and the perverted."

The man pursed his lips and nodded twice. "I'm impressed, Detective."

Phelps spat more blood at his shoes.

The man moved his foot away just in time. "Do you know why children are the prize they cherish the most?"

"You're drawn to their youth and innocence…" Phelps countered.

"Those things are just part of the overall equation."

"You and your kind are part of the equation!" Phelps sneered. "How can you participate in this? What the hell is wrong with you?"

"To serve is to be rewarded," he replied, smugly. "To oppose…"

"All for the procurement of one specific substance…"

"What is the substance we seek?" he scoffed as if Phelps would have no clue.

"Adrenochrome!"

"Goddamn it, Detective!" the man replied in excitement. "You are good." He looked at the table. "Killing you will cause me a good deal of sorrow."

"Are you even capable of sorrow?"

The man grumbled. He then went straight for the sharpening file on the table.

Phelps knew he had little time remaining. "Adrenal secretions, right?" Young children in a state of terror secrete massive doses of adrenaline into their blood just before they die!" Phelps studied him for a reaction. None came. He knew the man had lost his humanity. The man's nostrils fluctuated. "You feed on it, right?" He spat at the floor.

The man leaned in toward him. "Yes, Detective…" He was salivating. His eyes rolled into the back of his head. "Loosh is *such* a rush!" It does things far beyond your limited under-standing…"

"You sick fucks!" Phelps shouted at him as if his words would slay him right then and there.

"Don't look so disturbed. It's been going on for millennia inside the very institutions you hold sacrosanct."

Phelps gawked. 'It couldn't be!'

""The act of communion is celebrated every Sunday—a flesh-eating, blood-drinking ritual which billions of people willingly participate in."

Phelps cringed.

"So, Detective, as you can plainly see, you and the rest of the blind 'believers' are the real *sick fucks…*"

Phelps' face shriveled like he had just been sprayed by a skunk. "Adrenochrome is a drug to you… an addiction."

The man smirked. "Indeed, it is." He held the sharpen-ing tool in his thumb and forefinger and wrapped his arms across his chest, so he could see it clearly. "Putting the pieces of the puzzle together, are you?"

Phelps closed his eyes. 'I'd give everything to go one on one to the death with this man, squarely and fairly,' he thought to himself.

"What are your sources?"

"You use Child Protective Services, Amber Alerts and Juvenile Courts to expedite child trafficking. I am so on to you!"

"Who do you think the aforementioned 'services' actu-ally protect?"

"Your entire Satanic network, that's who!" Phelps roared, spittle flying everywhere. He shouted as if his reverberations could shatter the walls of the room he was in, "*That's what!*"

"You *are* on to us, but it is not *us* who actually benefit from this…"

"Who then?" Phelps barked

The man inhaled calmly and deftly rolled the instrument around in his fingers. "You detective ... are nothing more than a babe in the woods who has lost his way."

Phelps rocked and shook in his chair, doing anything he could to free himself.

"You are touching only the tip of the iceberg, Detective."

Phelps, realizing his predicament, slouched over in his chair. He had to conserve his strength in case somehow, some way, he got even an inch of slack in the ropes.

"Do you actually think the fluoridated, brain-dead public would ever believe something so..." The man paused before continuing. "...sadistic and bizarre as human sacrifice and the consumption of their flesh and blood?"

"That's how you've been getting away with it for so long!"

The man wrapped the sharpening tool in his open palm. "You rely on ignorance."

"Detective... you have no idea the way the world you live in actually works."

"I know more than you think I do and I'm learning more every minute." He spat. "Keep talking."

The man laughed. "Sadly, for you, you'll not benefit from a thing you're learning here today."

"Oh, I am already," Phelps replied, with growing confidence.

The man flicked the blade end up and clutched it tightly. "And... my stalwart Detective, you will never leave this room alive..."

Phelps rocked in his chair to loosen his bonds.

The man said, coldly, "Your body will never be discovered." He maneuvered around behind him, the blade reflecting the overhead fluorescent light. "And so, Detective... this is... your end."

Phelps began panting. He heard the omniscient voice

behind him overpowering and drowning out whatever the man was saying. "There is no end, Danny," he said calmly.

The man smiled deviously at Phelps. "We will torture you over and over until you are barely alive and the masters shall savor the flavor of your terror-infused blood until there is but one drop left to drink!"

The man brought his face within inches of Phelps' face.

"When your body can endure no more, it'll go up in flames. All of the knowledge you've worked so hard to accumulate will be nothing more than a series of lost, disjointed memories drifting aimlessly in the ether..."

Phelps lunged at him as best he could. "You're devils, not men!" he roared from the core of his soul.

The man jumped back, startled. He then snarled and struck Phelps with the back of his hand. He walked to the table and picked up the heavier, sturdier mallet. "I really don't care who you are or why you've come this far..." He coiled his fist around the wooden handle. "It's all meaningless now." He raised the mallet high overhead in preparation to strike. "I'm going to torture you anyway." He smiled, wickedly. "Because... your suffering... brings me... pleasure." He tightened his grip. "It brings... the masters... pleasure..."

Phelps whipped his head around fast enough to see the second man maneuver the chisel against Phelps' middle finger, but he knew he could do nothing. The mallet came down in a blur and struck the chisel. Phelps' lengthy, agony-filled scream and the ringing sounds of colliding metal filled the room in a cruel-sounding cacophony. The men merely laughed at him.

Just when he thought he could endure no more, Phelps felt the being's radiant hands on his shoulders. Phelps now sensed that this enigmatic man was some form of 'inner guide' rather than a stranger because he was not only leaning over Phelps' head in a protective manner, but he also seemed to know everything about him. He was also, despite his current predicament, reassuring him that he would be alright. He seemed to hear whispering in his ear: "Your thoughts have shaped your life, Danny. You are becoming what you think... what you feel." Phelps understood while allowing those words of comfort to block out the pain. "When your mind is pure, the essence of Who You Truly Are will shine forth and transmute the shadow self into blinding light that will never dim, once it has been activated."

Phelps felt the hands move away and he was curious when he then saw the spiritual form walking about the room, gazing at the ceiling; reaching out toward the walls and stopping before the display of cruel instruments on the table before him. Phelps was intuitively guided to focus his attention on the second man who stood nearby as the interrogator returned the chisel and mallet to the table in favor of another weapon. Phelps was then was suddenly overcome with a series of images from... inside... that man's very own mind. Their eyes locked. Phelps reeled back, intuitively knowing what that man knew. "Ah, we're hundreds of feet beneath the surface of the earth in a... military base." Phelps couldn't believe it. But it was sadly true. His mind was being overcome by things that he, before this very day, would have been impossible for him to believe. "They've been working with extraterrestrials against their own fellow man!" Phelps winced. He turned his head left. "Genetic experiments." He turned his head right. "DNA manipulation." He rocked his head back. "Mind control." Phelps gritted his teeth. "We're nothing but rats in their laboratory."

As Phelps probed the man's mind further, the man's hypnotized expression allowed Phelps to understand that this newly-developed power he was using against him could not be thwarted. The man could not seem to divert his eyes away from him or to break free from Phelps' mesmerizing gaze. Everything else around them seemed to become frozen in time.

"This is the control center that keeps humanity imprisoned and enslaved. An electromagnetic grid surrounds Earth, shunting the innate vibrational frequencies of human thought and behavior and blocking out our connection with our highest awareness and with our Creator. This is the heart of their control."

The man gasped suddenly.

"What's wrong?" the other snapped.

The man clutched his temple region. "He's probing my mind!"

"How?"

"He knows my thoughts!"

The other panicked.

"He knows everything!" His eyes shot daggers. "Kill him!"

The other snatched a long blade from the tray and lunged at Phelps.

* * *

Phelps discovered himself standing near the shore of a pristine waterfall. The mist moved over him, splattering him with droplets of cleansing water at precisely the perfect temperature to soothe and calm him further. Phelps looked around himself slowly and was immediately taken in by the astounding beauty surrounding him. He felt warm moisture under his outstretched palm and regarded a majestic lioness reaching up and under his hand so as to nuzzle up to him. He noticed how the finger that had been recently mauled was perfectly formed and uninjured. He stroked the cat's head and felt her psychically calling for her young to join them. Phelps turned his head slightly to see two youthful cubs bounding through the tall, swaying grass toward them.

He was then surrounded by brilliant, electric colors with a metallic sheen, far brighter than anything found in ordinary nature on Earth. The gentle sound of rushing water and the rhythmic sounds of the purring lioness melded together in perfect unity. The songs of nearby birds blended dreamily until everything was one perfect harmony. 'This is the way life was intended,' Phelps thought to himself.

He knew intuitively that human beings once lived as gods and goddesses in perfect harmony and oneness with the Universal Creator.

Phelps pondered that profound insight which rang as truth to him, for he felt overtaken by bliss. He noticed his beloved soulmate standing in the distance beneath a waterfall, with her hands outstretched, beckoning him while energetically threading her fingers through her hair. Phelps willed his translucent silvery clothing to fall away from his body and then walked toward the pool of water separating him from his beloved. He walked headlong into the warm, rejuvenating water without hesitating to test the temperature. He knew it would be absolutely perfect. He locked eyes with her and swam to her side, eagerly. When Phelps arrived a moment later, they gazed into one another's eyes with radiant clarity. It was a dance in perfect union with Universal Consciousness.

The waterfall cascaded over their intertwined bodies half-submerged in the deliciously-warm water. She wrapped her legs around him as he moved his waist into hers. Phelps emitted short, powerful and excited breaths as he approached her. He inhaled her fragrant scent and upon exhaling, he pressed his lips against hers, sharing his vital life force essence with her. A subtle wind rode in and tousled her long, black shiny hair, sending it brushing against Phelps' chiseled chest. They shared a laugh together, a deeply-satisfying laugh that seemed like it could last an entire lifetime and more.

She arched back in his arms and lay flush against the water which rolled in over her firm, perfectly-rounded breasts and erect nipples. She moaned in ecstasy. Then she leaned back up, smiled hungrily at him and pressed her breasts up against his chest. She raised her slender hand up and caressed Phelps' face before she opened her mouth ever so slightly and leaned in to kiss him. They gazed into one another's eyes with a feeling of complete Oneness, a rapture where the lovers transcended the physical and embraced the august, eternal, immortal power of their combined souls.

As their physical bodies were entwined, their energetic bodies merged. This union was far beyond the mortal lovemaking that Phelps had grown accustomed to on Earth.

The orgasmic waves they created resonated throughout this paradise, felt by all living creatures there without even engaging in the physical act of what he knew love making to be. There could be no comparison.

Chapter 14

PHELPS FLINCHED WHEN he realized he had been plucked out of the paradise he was enjoying so immensely and was instead seated in his Z06 Corvette back in the third-dimensional reality he knew so well.

When he regained his bearings, he found that he was leisurely cruising along a country road with miles of meadow on both sides of him. The day was remarkably clear and vibrant, though Phelps knew that no light on Earth could ever compare to the august majesty of the place he had just left. Earth suddenly felt like a cheap copy of what he instinctively now knew to be the real place where he came from and the place which, in the collective hearts of humanity, we all yearn to return.

He turned to his right to glance at the shimmering form sitting there quietly in the passenger seat regarding him with a broad smile. Phelps was becoming more and more accustomed to his presence and more open to the interaction. He now knew he was some kind of messenger, some type of inner guide. He knew the man, or being, *or whatever it was*, meant him no harm. In fact, the opposite rang true. He finally understood that he was here to help.

"So, if I understand this correctly," Phelps said aloud, allowing himself to contemplate.

The man smiled brightly.

"What you're trying to tell me is that... you're God?"

He had a glowing presence around him and Phelps could not help but think of the halo which surrounded Christ and other Saints and religious figures either worshipped or adored through the many ages of the world. "You're getting very close, Danny."

Phelps felt a warmth inside him.

"I am a light-bearing energy of Infinite Consciousness."

"Infinite," Phelps added. "No beginning..." He maneuvered the car around a bend. "No end."

"Precisely."

Phelps nodded. "What's happening to me?"

"You are awakening," the man replied, extending his open palm before the windshield. "You are seeing through the veil that separates your third-dimensional reality from other dimensions, other... realities."

Phelps could not contest any of it. He had experienced more than enough to know that what the man was telling him was in fact true. It had to be. Phelps came to the sudden, startling realization that it was he, not the man, who had dimensionally-shifted himself from the chair in the base he had been confined in and placed himself instead into a paradise beyond words. *"But how,"* he thought, *"how is this new-found ability possible?"* He had to ask the most glaringly obvious question. *"What* are you?"

"I am an expression of Universal Consciousness. I simply... AM!"

After all that had transpired, Phelps was surprised that his reply seemed too much to understand.

"I am an extension, an expression of Universal Consciousness. I am a tiny portion of something far greater and like you, I am in a constant process of self-discovery. I am an individuated aspect or expression of the All That Is. I am light and through the power of free will, I am entering the darkness to bring about light... the dawn of a new golden age for humanity."

Phelps studied him curiously.

"You mean like walking into a dark room and turning the light on? The darkness is suddenly gone. Like that?"

The man smiled warmly. "Yes. I am the Kingdom of God within you."

Phelps nodded as the words began to make sense at last.

"Everyone and everything in the Universe are an extension of the glorious whole. Humanity is an experiment that I am intricately involved with." He smiled. "Do you understand?"

"I..." Phelps replied. "I don't know..." He contemplated and stared out the front windshield in awe at the prospect. "How long have you been doing this?"

"Since the dawn of creation."

Phelps expected an answer like that. "And what is your next adventure?"

"I'm going to sojourn through this wondrous universe, the same thing I'm doing now, really. Growing, evolving, expressing consciousness..."

"What about me?" Phelps interrupted. "What part do I play in all of this?"

"This is our collective journey. We are in this *together*."

"I don't know about this journey. I quite frankly was having a lot of fun before you showed up!" he said, gruffly.

"I've always been with you, Danny. I share every thought, every experience, every feeling, every expression of Who You Are."

Phelps gasped silently. He remembered how he was able to read the thoughts of the interrogator in the military base through an act of his own will and how easily that took place. He recoiled at the prospect that the strange being now seated beside him could read his thoughts just as easily, and experience his private life as if it were theirs to share mutually.

"Did you think your life would never change? Look how it's changing now."

"Oh, it's changing alright," Phelps chuckled and scoffed simultaneously.

"Don't get too comfortable, Danny..."

Phelps was taken aback for a split second.

"Change always beckons us when it is needed most and also when we least expect it."

Phelps shifted his eyes from the road long enough to stare intently at the man beside him.

"Look at what you have survived. Do not fear death. When you realize there really is no death, then you can do anything, because there's nothing to fear. People in *presumed* positions of power have told you all your life what you could or could not do, right?"

"You've got that right."

"What a clever deception it is to convince the all-powerful that they have no power at all."

"Your parents sent you to school to learn math and science, and instead, they handed you their version of reality. They taught you that you are nothing, when in reality, you are everything. You are part of Creator's infinite, perfect design. You are a part of All That Is. You are all that was, all that is and all that ever shall be."

Phelps nodded. "That's beginning to make sense." He was eager to learn about these other creatures he had seen in his visions. "Tell me, what other expressions of life have you assumed?"

"I have personally expressed as both male and female in bodies that originated from every region of the world. I've been rich beyond avarice. I've been among the poorest of the poor. I've studied diligently in the tallest mountains as a monk in Tibet, and as a Jewish rabbi huddled in a small room studying the Torah by candlelight. I've been a philosopher, a stalwart warrior, and a helpless slave. I've been the most celebrated athlete in the world and the most pitied cripple. I've been loved. I've been aborted before I was ever born. I've lived in castles and I've left my physical body as a penniless pauper. I've lived lives with 15 wives and others with varying numbers of homosexual lovers all of whom meant the world to me, but whom I have had to hide from my family out of fear of rejection or ridicule. I've murdered and I have been murdered. I've now evolved to the point where I do everything in my great power to celebrate life by saving lives instead of snuffing them out."

Phelps smiled.

"The list goes on..."

"Damn, why did you do all of that to yourself?"

"To express my own uniqueness as I experience Creation, of course..."

Phelps nodded. "Of course." He chuckled aloud.

"When I am finished with this universe, I will simply transfer my awareness to another."

"Another... universe?" Phelps was confused.

"There is more than this one universe," he added.

Phelps lifted his hands from the steering wheel and held them up before him as if he could take no more.

"We don't live in a single universe, Danny."

"We don't?"

"Would that not limit the Creator?" He smiled intensely. "I've told you, there is no beginning and no end, haven't I?"

"We exist across all space, time, and dimensions in a multiverse containing an infinite number of universes."

"C'mon," Phelps protested. "How can there be unlimited universes?"

The man giggled. "Each of us will eventually create our own universe."

Phelps mocked him. "I'm going to create universes, am I?"

"Of course," he replied. "Are you not an individuated aspect of All That Is?"

"Yes?" he replied, questioning the reply rather than making any form of bold statement which he knew to be absolutely true.

"Yes, you certainly are. When you truly understand the scope of what that means, you'll then know that you are a god in the early stages of development. Because all cells divide to become exactly like their host cell, you, the divine expression currently incarnated as Danny Phelps, will become just like the Creator."

"This is too much." Phelps lifted a hand from the steering wheel and rubbed his forehead.

"The truth will eventually set you free."

"Well," Danny replied. "That's nothing I haven't heard before," he laughed. "Especially... in my line of work."

"You have plenty of evolving to do until you get to that point. Billions of years in fact, as you decode time in your earthly reality."

Phelps coughed.

"But, because you have no end, you'll eventually get it right. You have no beginning and no end, remember?"

"Are *you* alone in this adventure?"

"Of course not. We are never alone."

Phelps' eyes grew wider in anticipation of what profound words would come next.

"We have soulmates."

"My soulmate," Phelps blurted out. "The woman!"

"Yes, she has been patiently waiting for you as you experience this earthly experience."

Phelps wrinkled his brow.

"And…" the man added.

Phelps pondered the thought until his eyes reddened and he could no longer hold back tears.

"Alex…"

"Yes, Alex is also one of your soulmates."

"I have finally found peace."

"I know!" Unconditional forgiveness is crucial. Alex chose his lifetime, even before he was born. Just as you did. He chose to be your catalyst for change. He did it solely because of his deep love for you. He willingly surrendered his brief life so that you would become… who you needed to become."

Phelps' eyes overflowed with tears. It was all too difficult to bear, but he knew, in the seat of his soul, that no greater truth was being spoken.

"And because of that gesture, your destiny is now unfolding, precisely as it was meant to."

Phelps wiped away his tears and sobbed. "I don't know what that means." He wept. "I just can't believe that the bad decisions I've made in my life contribute to my overall destiny and that they benefit me."

"Don't be so hard on yourself, Danny. Don't judge yourself. I don't judge you."

Phelps felt cold. He felt deep down that he had done completely awful things to himself and to others in his brief sojourn here.

"I totally accept and love you unconditionally."

Phelps wept so hard, he nearly lost control of the car. He felt his abdomen convulsing as he cried from the deepest recesses of his soul. Anguish overcame him and when he felt the man's hand on his shoulder, it was all washed away like a wave of warm honey crashed over him.

"I love you *that* you are, not for what you do or do not do. I love you simply because you exist."

Phelps wept.

"I love you because Creator made you precisely the way you are."

"Why?"

"So Creator could experience itself, express itself, and discover itself."

"I don't understand..."

"Through you, Danny!"

Phelps gasped.

"Creator experiences itself through individuated expressions of itself going out into the great, limitless Multiverse, exploring all space, time, and dimensions, to grow and to evolve, and to become."

"Become?" It was the question that had eaten at his soul every waking day of his life to date. "Become... *what*?"

The man smiled as brightly as ever. "Your destiny."

Phelps' eyes dried as he sat with that for several long minutes and came to terms with it.

When he was recharged, he turned to query further and asked, "What's next?"

"Are you ready to find out?"

"I... AM!" Phelps beamed."

The tachometer read 7000 RPM when Phelps popped the clutch, downshifted, and jammed his foot upon the accelerator. The tires burned brief, clean, even lines on the pavement and the car roared down the road.

"YEE-HAA!"

He was always one to put on a show, if the timing and the opportunity had both presented themselves.

The inner-guide smiled at him.

For the first time in a great long while, he was ready to stand in his own newly-found power.

Phelps grinned as he cranked up the music and the song *'Renegade'* by the band Styx blasted through the speakers. Phelps suddenly felt more alive and more energized than ever before. This strange being, this otherworldly *'friend,'* had somehow unlocked the place inside him which allowed his long-suppressed dignity and honor to finally be set free. Most empowering of all, Phelps could now sense a newfound purpose, an unfolding destiny that he had never believed possible at this stage of his life.

Through the windshield, a meadow came into full view and the inner guide pointed a finger out the side window. Phelps eased off the accelerator and lowered the volume on the sound system. The car slowed to a rumbling crawl as he did his best to follow the man's finger. It pointed toward a blurred, shadowy-gray form that was shifting and moving along the edge of the meadow where it met the line of trees in the forest beyond.

"Is that what I think it is?"

In the time that he had, Phelps studied the bizarre-looking creature as it moved along the tree line.

"Seek and ye shall find..."

"Let's check it out!" Phelps said.

Phelps pulled off the road to conceal his car as best he could. He was tired of playing games, tired of being on the defensive. It was time to use his finely-honed skills for some serious payback.

Phelps turned off the engine and his inner guide was nowhere to be seen. Phelps leaned over and popped open the glove box. Inside, he saw the top edge of his Glock 23 handgun. He pulled it out, flipped it around until he held the grip firmly in his hand, and checked the magazine. Within but a moment, he was out of the car and closing the door, scanning the tree line ahead of him.

With gun in hand, Phelps moved down the embankment

and cut through the grassy meadow, crouching most of the way, stealthily stalking the creature he had seen ahead of him. He seemed to feel his immaterial guide keeping pace behind him, but he wasn't exactly sure. He knew, this time, he was meant to take matters into his own experienced hands.

Once he had come close enough, he ducked when he saw that the individual creature he had seen earlier had now joined two others and they all seemed to be looking back in Phelps' general direction.

After several long and dreadful moments, they turned around and disappeared into the trees, seemingly uninterested or altogether unconcerned with Phelps' presence.

As he took his first step into the forest, Phelps realized that the path he was taking was a search for truth and the larger questions of purpose and of existence and how one defines the dichotomy of good versus evil. Less than a week ago, he wouldn't have given any thought at all to the existence of any universal truth, but now, here in the place where he could very well lose his life, Phelps was becoming more and more convinced that there was indeed a higher purpose to his life after all.

Phelps stepped into a grove which consisted of several dozen trees, running east-west for about 40 yards and more than three times that in width. The stone-littered ground was slightly sloped and blanketed with fallen leaves and scraggly patches of grass. He stopped and cocked an ear to listen.

After a brief moment, he thought he heard something. He moved but a few more paces and spun around in a wide circle. Then, he was sure of it. Eerily familiar, faint screams of pure terror echoed off the trees from some place deeper in the forest. Phelps shuddered, because this time, the screams did not come from the lips of a child, like they had earlier, but from what sounded like a struggling female teenager in considerable pain. Phelps ground his teeth, fixed his eyes ahead of him and pressed on.

As he moved through the thicket, he felt a stagnating invisible weight about the area as he stumbled upon the same familiar stone altar.

'How?' Phelps begged. He was beginning to question his own sanity.

He knew that he was not in the same spot as had been before, yet here stood the very same altar he had visited, both in his visions and in his physical body.

He studied the thick, coarse, chiseled slab that functioned as its base. Then, his eyes moved gradually upward to the roughly-hewn granite block in the center, and finally to the smooth polished surface of the altar itself. He brushed a few fallen leaves away and traced his finger around the arcane symbols carved along its length which were either painted black or more likely covered in some form of pitch from other ceremonies or burnt offerings that had been practiced at that location.

Phelps turned around as another scream filled his heart with dread and foreboding. He slowly peeled his fingers away from the evil symbols and felt a stickiness on the tips, forcing him to flick his wrist as if to cast off any lingering negative energies he might have interacted with. He would have normally made fun of such an absurd action, but given the recent events, and his increased sensitivities, he knew that subtle energies were not only real, but they were important things to be aware of.

As Phelps continued, pale sunlight cast long shadows through the tree branches and speckled the ground before him, shining orange among the many fallen leaves. Low walls made of perfectly piled stone defined the outer perimeter of what Phelps determined to be authentic sacrificial grounds.

He had read about such places, heard about them from first-hand accounts of women who had claimed to have escaped ritual Satanic abuse, but never in his wildest dreams would he have actually believed he'd be setting foot in one. The whole concept was too much to bear, too far-fetched to believe.

Now he knew, however, that denial such as his, *and on the part of the whole of humanity*, was precisely what had allowed it to go on for so long, hidden in the shadows of perpetual twilight.

And so, courage drove him onward. Though his intense fear was evident, he noticed his rapidly pounding heart and the short, shallow breaths he was struggling with.

Phelps made his way down a steep, winding path, into some denser trees and finally into the shadow of a protective oak. There, he remained hidden and the screams grew louder. Each of his nerve endings were firing on hyper-alert, as he struggled hard to maintain his composure. He knew that one slip-up would spell certain doom, both for himself and the girl. Phelps cringed. He began to suffer the effects of what could only be described as 'sensory overload.' Phelps found himself embroiled in a situation far outside the realm of possibility, and it was taking its toll. He had to keep reminding himself that what he was experiencing was unlike anything he had ever before imagined, a reality-shattering nightmare that was choking him like a cloud of noxious fumes.

Phelps took three short, powerful breaths through his nostrils before he finally summoned the courage to peek around the tree to take his first look.

There, as expected, in the distance, back to the ground, lay a young woman, barely out of her teens, screaming and violently tugging her arms and legs away from two menacing men struggling to gain control of her.

Every impulse would have normally sent Phelps rushing

to her rescue. He wanted to intervene, truly, but his own growing terror exacerbated by the Reptilian presence over-powered his intention to take action. Phelps turned quickly to look at her again. Her crestfallen expression stabbed deep into his heart. He retracted and leaned his head back against the tree. Were it merely a pair of twisted perverts he needed to confront, he would have leapt right into action, but he was well aware that the Reptilians lurking somewhere nearby in the forest were by far, the more sinister and powerful threat.

Phelps squatted low and peered around the tree. Then was when he saw them, two more Reptilians, their bodies perfectly cloaked in some form of an opaque blackness phas-ing into the forest like creeping shadows.

As the seconds moved onward, Phelps blinked repeat-edly. With each brief flick of his eyelids, the Reptilians seemed to shift more clearly into focus, from something thoroughly immaterial into something tangible, physical.

Phelps analyzed the threat.

There they stood, motionless, directly behind the pair of human predators as they tried their best to subdue the wily young woman. Their bodies were immense, and ripped with corded muscle, with not an ounce of fat to be seen. Their many scales were now green and glistening. The yellow claws at the end of their toes dug into the soil as they moved a full step closer toward the men and planted their bare feet firmly on the ground. The men who were busily subduing the girl paid the Reptilians no attention whatsoever. Phelps didn't understand that at all. Then he thought about the human male standing side-by-side with the Reptilians in the base where he was being tortured earlier. He knew, by now, they were all working together, 'but when had such a sinis-ter alliance been formed between the foulest of humankind and these strange, otherworldly creatures?' he wondered.

Phelps gasped. What he saw next gnawed at his heart

like a bloodthirsty animal. He could do nothing but stare hopelessly and watch the black, translucent swirling clouds forming in the Reptilians' abdominal regions and out of each of them, came a smoking, phantasmal tentacle which lashed out wildly toward the men. Then, Phelps lurched back. The appendages flayed forward like striking cobras and latched onto the back of each man like they had both been skewered by some metaphysical hooks.

The men seemed unfazed.

'Are you kidding me?' Phelps thought.

The Reptilians were somehow, Phelps discerned, now determinedly attached to the human men with what appeared to be thick shadowy cords, now contracting and expanding like hoses as if they were... feeding. Phelps gagged. He turned back around, scraped his back on the bark of the tree and slid down until his weight was firmly supported by the thick, exposed roots. He could take no more of it. That was, until he heard the sounds, the slurping and gulping sounds overpowering all of the natural sounds of the forest with their unnatural, preternatural reverberations.

Filled with dread, Phelps moved in even closer with slow and quiet precision, doing his best so as not to be discovered.

The girl's screams intensified and as they did so, Phelps beheld a wispy black cloud form perfectly over the girl like a shadowy outline overlaying her trembling body. As he gazed in horror, it appeared that the mist ever-so-slowly moved off and away from her toward the Reptilians and into the cores of their torsos.

"Get ahold of her fucking feet, goddamn it!" called the man now kneeling behind her head, struggling with her arms.

The man at her feet wound his hand inside the ends of her jeans and balled the fabric up in his fist, holding both of her legs as securely as he could with one hand as she repeatedly kicked her legs out. The other man let go of her arms, quickly spun around, straddled her chest and pinned her biceps firmly to the ground with his knees. She screamed in protest and at the pain now radiating down her arms. As the man at the girl's feet unbuttoned his own pants, the girl screeched and managed to yank her legs free of his grasp. Then, astonishing her attacker, she kicked him in both the jaw and throat, sending him reeling back into the brush.

The other man spun around as best he could to see what had happened. "Get the fuck over here. I'm losing her!" Little did he know that he unintentionally eased up on the pressure against her right arm, enough for her to free it and crack her fist across his cheek with a vicious growl. As she did so, her ring cut into him and tore a gash in his face.

"Ahh..." the man screamed, pressing his palm against his cheek. Once he'd peeled his hand away, he checked his palm and noticed a few drops of blood from where her ring had gouged him. "Now you've done it!"

The girl spun away, rolling over and over in the leaves until she was safely clear of him. The second she got to her feet, though, he was rushing toward her, but she kicked him square in the groin at precisely the right moment.

His surprise was soon overwhelmed by the shooting, burning pain in his groin. He crumpled to the ground and curled up into the fetal position. "Ahh, you dirty bitch!" he moaned.

As Phelps watched, the Reptilians standing there arched their backs and raised their palms to waist level as if they were soaking up the conflict and feasting upon it as Phelps had surmised. Their gizzards undulated and if that weren't revolting enough, they produced a gulping and swishing sound that again began to turn Phelps' stomach sour.

The young woman crouched low to gain her bearings, scanning the forest with panic-stricken eyes for some route of escape. Little did she know that the man she'd kicked in the face previously had already recovered and was preparing to strike. She moved a few paces and to Phelps' complete astonishment, she passed straight through an unresponsive Reptilian.

The man exiting the brush called out, "Get that bitch, goddamn it, don't let her get away!"

As she tried to escape, the man on the ground tripped her up and she fell face-first into the leaves. The man coming out of the brush then leapt on top and straddled her just as his compatriot did earlier. The young woman spun around and desperately raked at his face with her fingernails. The man's face contorted as she gouged him over and over, digging her nails into his vulnerable flesh as deeply as she could.

"You bitch!"

The man flailed his arms before his face and batted her hands away, managing to grab her by the wrists and pin them down long enough for him to slide up further and secure her into submission.

She struggled helplessly as he glared down at her. The blood from his recent wounds dripped down and splattered her face. The man laughed and raised a powerful fist and held it aloft to torment her. "You shouldn't have done that, missy." The last thing she saw were the fine, wiry black hairs on his knuckles before his fist came down against her jaw, knocking her instantly into the hazy realm just outside of consciousness. He caressed her rapidly swelling face with the pad of his thumb and then worked his hand inside her blouse. As the other man limped toward her, still cupping his crotch, he tugged violently on her blouse, popping off many of the pearlescent buttons which rolled away into the leaves. She struggled but could do nothing against the weight pressing down on her arms. She growled like a vicious dog and lunged her head up as she stabbed at him with her eyes. But that was all she could do.

The other man spat on the ground. "Yeah, that's what I'm talking about. Now let's show this bitch how we do things in the back woods."

The man holding the girl down regarded his partner's heavily breathing. "Get her fucking pants off!" He pulled off his belt and whipped the young woman in the face. She whelped in response.

As Phelps silently observed, the Reptilians seemed to be experiencing some form of ecstatic *pleasure* as one of the human males started to really subdue her. Once she screamed aloud, the Reptilians appeared to relish it even more so as the negative energy began to multiply.

When Phelps looked again, he noticed, much to his horror and shock, that one of the Reptilians stepped closer toward her. Even though its eyes remained tightly closed, it seemed to know precisely what was taking place around it. Phelps followed it with his eyes as it raised an arm. Then, it sent a single, hooked claw down into the soft space between her shoulder and clavicle with a ferocious flash, piercing her soft, pink flesh and digging deeper into both tendon and bone, sending a shiver of agony through her torn shoulder which intensified her terror. The girl wailed in anguish from the unseen attack.

With her energy fast being depleted, she struggled and screamed into the barren trees.

"Nobody can hear your screams out here," he said as he unfastened the button securing her jeans.

He stroked her firm thighs back and forth. He tugged violently at her zipper and worked himself up into a state of pure ecstasy. Adrenaline coursed through his veins as he began to pull down her jeans.

The thoroughly exhausted girl turned her head away from her assailant and whispered a last faint desperate plea. "Help me. Somebody... please help me."

"We'll help you, girl," assured the man who had her pinned down. "Don't worry, it'll all be over soon."

The girl could fight no longer and surrendered to her fate.

Phelps knew that she'd gnaw his balls right off if only she could reach them.

Still hidden behind the tree, Phelps was nearly hyperventilating, summoning his courage. He held his Glock 23 firmly in his hands and pressed the sight at the far top edge of the gun barrel to his lips. He didn't want to be killed no sooner than he came into view. He closed his eyes in prayer and whispered to himself, "Oh God, protect me as I take up your sword and drop these sub-human dirt bags!"

"I will never leave you!" Phelps looked around and could see nothing, but the message seemed to echo in his mind.

Phelps dug his fingers into the bark of the tree. In a flash, he saw himself as the 11-year-old boy he once was, courageously unsheathing his father's samurai sword to save his beloved brother, Alex, and scared to death at the same time to face an adversary more than three times his size. This time, in this place, Phelps decided he would act in time to save the girl and make amends for failing to do so in time to save his older brother.

The horrific terror the girl exuded; the twisted violence of the men and the undulating ecstasy of the foul Reptilians culminated into a crescendo of dark and evil energy, void of all light.

Phelps wrapped his palm around the tree and dug the heel of his boot against the roots. Every muscle in his body fired. He felt his soul reach out and empower his third-dimensional body. Phelps whispered, "Alex!"

In spite of all of his own fears and doubts, Phelps leaped out from behind the tree to confront the two slack-jawed men who saw him come out of nowhere. Phelps shot his hands forward and aimed his gun at them. His eyes widened. "Freeze, goddamn it!"

Though the men were shocked, the Reptilians were totally unresponsive. They seemed, instead, much to Phelps' disgust, to be soaking in the energies of the conflict with even more unbridled enthusiasm than before.

"Let her go!" Phelps shouted. "Now!" His words echoed off the surrounding trees.

The men sprung open their palms and moved slowly off and away from her, crouching and groveling on the ground before him.

The young woman rolled over onto her hands and knees. She gasped in an effort to regain her breath. She stared in disbelief at her savior for a moment and screamed, "Shoot them!"

The Reptilians sucked in the very ether around them like babes on a nipple. Phelps aimed at the men and then at the Reptilians. The Reptilians were not the immediate threat, he knew, so he aimed again at the two astonished men. Phelps' fear was palpable as he exchanged uneasy glances between his four enemies.

When Phelps aimed again at the Reptilians, the men reached behind their backs in unison and withdrew their handguns, but before they even came close to pointing them in Phelps' direction, a dozen popping noises echoed off the trees and they both crumpled to their sides in a spray of their own blood.

Phelps clutched his handgun in his fist and narrowed his eyes while focusing on the Reptilians. The gray smoke rose up from gun's muzzle and wafted up into the trees and into the early evening sky. The creatures seemed like they had climaxed just when he cut the men down. Now that the violence had dissipated, they stood there, motionless as if the fear buffet they had been feasting on had run dry.

The girl's sobs forced Phelps to turn and regard her.

'It's time to act,' Phelps knew, '...before they become a more potent and present threat.'

Phelps swiped his thumb over the release lever, allowing gravity to expel the spent magazine which fell onto the ground and disappeared into the fallen leaves. He reached behind him and unbuttoned the black leather pouch on his hip, fishing out a fresh clip, sliding it into the gun, and snapping it firmly into place. He stood in shock before an evil, foreign presence, but he felt comforted while cocking a round into the chamber. The hollow-point bullets were the best weapons he had available. He hoped and prayed they would be good enough. He drew a series of deep breaths and pointed his gun at the Reptilians. He shouted at them with authority, "You freeze right there, you sick fucks!"

Startled, one of the creatures popped open its eyes, turned, and fixed its sinister gaze upon him. Even though it was far from human, Phelps could read its astonished expression as easily as he had learned to read any human's. Phelps moved to the side to regard the other Reptilian who had also snapped out of its state of ecstasy. It too was also obviously spooked. They blinked in unison, their green eyelids closing around their marble-like eyes, not from the top or bottom, but from the left and right sides. Phelps lurched back, rattled. The way it blinked was so... alien, so... disturbing, Phelps was briefly paralyzed. The creatures then looked at each other in dismay. Before he could even swing his sidearm into position, the Reptilians sped into the woods in a dull, gray flash faster than he would ever have believed possible.

Phelps sprang into action. He shouted ahead of him while brandishing his weapon, "I said... freeze!" Phelps pulled the trigger over and over as they ran together through the dense forest. The first three bullets, he knew, struck the lead Reptilian squarely in center of its back. He nodded in satisfaction. The fourth and fifth bullets blasted off bits of bark from two separate trees as the Reptilians deftly maneuvered between them.

Phelps entered a clearing and drove his feet into the fallen leaves. He had a clean shot. He raised his gun to eye level and hammered them both in the back with five more rounds. To his astonishment, the bullets passed straight through them, as if they were not even there. Phelps passed a hand before his face which was locked in an expression of shock and horror as two more Reptilians came out of a thicket and joined the others. They exchanged uneasy glances and three of them streaked off out of sight. The fourth, however, planted its foot on the ground and turned back to observe its pursuer. There they stood, face to face, nemesis against nemesis, good versus evil. As it stood there, staring at him, its amber eyes glowed like distant suns against night's slowly encroaching darkness. He recognized that primal fear he had seen radiating from so many frightened perps he had nabbed on the streets. Phelps felt that it knew it had been discovered. As Phelps held his smoking handgun, he could do nothing more than stare back at the strange being. And then, it was off, passing as easily between the trees as does a summer breeze blow through the tall green grass of a meadow.

Phelps spun around, scanning the trees, relieved that he wasn't forced to engage the being with what he now understood to be a useless weapon. Furthermore, he felt an unnerving knot growing in his gut because he was unsure just how many more of the strange Reptilians were lurking somewhere within the forest.

* * *

Faint cries beckoned Phelps back into the valley where he found the young woman kneeling in the dirt, sobbing with her face held securely in her cupped hands. He had failed to stop the Reptilians, but at least he had saved her. The leaves crunched under his boots as he approached slowly. He stood there in a protective stance and then knelt down in front of her. She lunged on him and Phelps held her safely in his arms. She shook uncontrollably, the adrenaline still coursing through her veins.

"Everything's okay, sweetie. It's over now."

Moments passed as Phelps held her in his protective embrace. He scanned the surroundings. When she finally pulled back away from him, tears were streaming down her face. She looked into his eyes.

"What were you shooting at?"

Phelps regarded the dead men lying beside them. The look she gave him revealed that she was as deeply concerned as she was confused.

The girl shook her head and spoke softly, "No, not them."

Phelps gave her a quizzical look.

"You ran after something... shooting."

Phelps looked in the direction from which he came.

"What were you shooting at?"

Phelps had a moment of pristine clarity as he cupped his hand over the top of her head and stroked her hair. "Shh," he whispered. He came to the realization that through the entire ordeal, she had been unable to perceive the Reptilians as he did, because they were vibrating outside of her ability to perceive them. The pieces were all starting to fit together. It was all starting to make sense.

Phelps stood and extended his forearm for the girl to grab onto. She raised both hands and hooked them over his arm and he hoisted her up. He wrapped one arm around her shoulder and held one of her forearms securely.

When they made their way out of the valley and spotted Phelps' car, the blood red sun was moving down at its lowest angle, visible only through the lowest, scraggly branches of the distant trees. When they made it to the car, the first twin-kling stars became visible in the deepening darkness. Those stars, as Phelps was beginning to realize, were far more important to the affairs on earth than most anyone realized.

Now, the time is now... for humans to awaken to the lessons learned from the darkness and discover they are no longer children frolicking in the Garden.

Chapter 15

DETECTIVE PHELPS SAT pensively on a bar stool at the Lonestar Gentleman's Club, staring past the flickering television screen and the news channel thereon. His inner guide, indiscernible to all but himself, sat beside him, observing silently. Phelps held his chin in his palm with his fingers draped over his mouth and nose.

"Simney Chicon, reporting from Houston's NASA space center. I'm here with research scientist Dr. Sharan Patel who has discovered a fantastic event occurring right here in our very own Milky Way Galaxy, something that, quite possibly, will affect all life on earth."

Phelps widened his eyes. Nothing at all surprised him anymore. He seemed to be embroiled in a great galactic drama. He watched as the reporter started talking directly to the scientist in question.

"Doctor Patel, as we show your images to our viewers, please explain what is happening..."

The monitor revealed a massive explosion of light energy from the Galactic Core that radiated outward toward the Earth. The Indian doctor's accent was distinct.

"In 1987, 26,000 light years away, a massive explosion occurred in the center of the galaxy. The blast radius was 5,000 light years across. I have to tell you, to those that don't know the scope of this incredible event, that it is..." he chuckled to himself, "...simply mind-blowing."

Phelps frowned.

"An orbiting observatory detected this anomaly and recorded the flash of light just now becoming visible to us here on Earth. This light energy could possibly be the harbinger of a cataclysm unheard of in all of the history of our planet."

Phelps looked at his inner guide who sat beside him looking at the television with an amused expression.

"We split the light," Dr. Patel continued, "into its many different wavelengths and we've analyzed the data to determine its brightness and power."

Phelps laughed inside at the blank, dumbfounded expression on the reporter's face as she glanced back and forth into the camera.

"We have been tracking this ever since. It is..."

Phelps folded his hands on the bar and nodded.

The doctor continued, "...headed towards Earth." Proxima Centauri or Alpha Centauri C is a red dwarf Star in the Constellation Centaurus, 4.244 light years from our Sun. The light energy cast off from this flash is over 1,000 times brighter than the sun itself. It is literally out of this world!"

The reporter's eyes lit up, this was her chance to break the story of the century, possibly of all time. She arranged her hair neatly and asked, "When will it reach Earth?" She smiled brightly as if she had any clue what that would actually mean.

"It already has," the scientist said, coolly and with a great deal of concern.

The woman's eyes grew wide, unsure. She looked around her.

"The event horizon has been bombarding our solar system for a short time now. A precursor wave of this energy has already permeated Earth's magnetic shield."

Phelps looked over at his inner guide. He smirked and

nodded at him, ever so slightly. His telling glance afforded Phelps the confirmation that everything he had experienced thus far was not only real, but that it was just the beginning of what was to become an experience well beyond his wildest imaginings.

"What will happen?" the reporter asked.

"We really don't know how it will affect Earth. This light energy is nothing we have ever encountered before."

The reporter's concerned look was hard to conceal.

"However, we believe that the electromagnetic field that protects us from cosmic events such as this one will be a sufficient shield."

Luke flicked off the television because the group of friends all knew that Luke didn't particularly like to show stories that could or likely would upset his customers. People came there to escape their stressful lives and to relax and forget their worries, not add to them.

Phelps took a sip of his drink and held his glass firmly on the bar with both hands. He locked eyes with his inner guide who smirked and said, "I'm well aware that you have a thousand questions..."

Phelps practically spat out his drink. "And then some." He sucked down the last bit of bourbon. "Though, I don't really know where to begin..."

His inner guide raised a brow.

"What the hell was that all about in those woods?" Phelps continued.

"Well, for starters, you saved the life of a young girl who was facing a certain, horrifying death." He placed his hand on Phelps' shoulder and spun him around on his bar stool. Phelps nodded, gratefully. "When was the last time you've done that?"

"Never," Phelps blurted out. Not even as a cop." He wrinkled his forehead. "What exactly are those Reptilian looking things."

"You've never personally interacted with them before," his inner guide interjected.

"No, of course not!"

"Are you sure?" he looked at him quizzically.

"I'm sure," he said gruffly. He spun his glass around in circles. "I think I'd remember something like that." He looked up at his inner guide. "Don't you?"

"You'd think."

Phelps gave him a confused look. It was as if his inner guide was intentionally withholding something from him, information he would either be unable to understand at present or something he was not yet ready to deal with.

"They've always been here."

Phelps nearly fell backward off his bar stool. His brows raised high. "Excuse me?" he pressed. "Why didn't they react when I took out those two perps, like I wasn't even there?"

"They *did* react. They were in total shock when they realized that you had actually discovered them and more importantly... *what they were doing.*" They didn't pay you any attention, because they didn't think it was possible for you to enter their dimensional reality. They thought that you, like the rest of the surface population, were utterly unable to discern their presence."

Phelps whipped his head over toward Luke and tapped the rim of his empty glass. His nerves were firing in a way he hadn't experienced before and he needed another drink. He couldn't believe what he was hearing. He knew, as did everyone else that all people lived on the planet surface. Where else would they live? He turned to face his inner guide once again and asked, "*Surface* population?"

"There are civilizations far older and far more advanced than yours living within the honeycomb earth..."

Phelps pounded his fist on the bar and shot his inner guide a look of sheer frustration, "C'mon! Stop fucking with me!"

"You thought you were alone in this universe." The inner guide grinned from ear to ear. "You thought that the human race was the oldest and wisest civilization on earth?"

"Everyone knows that."

"Think again." He paused and continued, "Danny, you're going to find that much of what you have been led to believe is simply one convenient lie stacked upon an even deeper, more sinister lie to hide the true nature of reality from you."

Danny sat there and drew a deep breath and held it. When he had time to digest what he had just heard, he asked, "Back to the Reptilians, goddamn it. Why was I able to perceive those Reptilians when nobody else could? Why were they so taken off guard when they realized I could see them?"

"They didn't enter your world, you entered into a density very close to theirs! You could perceive them, and they you, but as you discovered, your bullets could not harm them."

"Here ya go, buddy," said the bartender, who lowered the mouth of the bourbon bottle until it clanked against the side of Phelps' empty glass. Phelps backed away and allowed Luke to pour as he digested what he had just been told. Phelps felt that unmistakable feeling that he was being spied on, so he spun around in his swiveling bar stool and spotted Terra looking at him while in the lap of an overweight, elderly man. She looked back at the man, licked the tip of her finger and ran it down the nose and lips of the undulating creep beneath her and sprang up from his lap. She smirked satisfactorily at the small tent that she had caused to rise in his khakis and then she sauntered over toward the bar.

"Hey, Danny, how are you doing? You want some company?"

His inner guide chuckled, "Do you want to part *company* with your money, is more like it."

Phelps responded in kind with a chuckle of his own. "No, that's okay, sweetie. Maybe later."

Terra looked somewhat dejected. "You okay, Danny?" She leaned lower so she could display more of her supple breasts as she continued pressing him. "You look like you're in some kind of deep contemplation or something."

Phelps' inner guide leaned in and said, "I'm always so fascinated with the profound intuition with which women are so gifted... truly connected."

Phelps looked at him briefly and turned again to face Terra. He then turned back toward his inner guide and said softly, "She's a sweet girl."

He eyed her fondly and winked. "I'm fine, Terra. I've just had a long day."

"Suit yourself," Terra replied, spinning on her heels and sashaying toward another customer.

"So back to those sadistic Reptilians," Phelps prodded his immaterial ally.

"Speak kindly of the dark ones, Danny."

Phelps lurched back. He couldn't believe his ears at first. He rapped his knuckles on the bar and laughed aloud. "What?" He took a swig of his drink.

"They're on their own evolutionary path, just as you are."

"But..." Phelps interjected. The inner guide cocked an ear to listen. "You saw them enjoying themselves at the expense of that poor girl's horror." He extended his hand. "You *did* see that, right?"

"Yes, I saw it. They derive pleasure from people's suffering. They feed off you... your fears, your anger, hatred, violence, discord, and a plethora of other negative emotions, both miniscule and intense, consuming it as one consumes food."

"A feeding-frenzy," Phelps nodded. He didn't want to believe it, but that is precisely what he determined what was happening in the woods.

"Human energy fuels them, gives them their much-needed sustenance, just like you nurture yourself with the kinds of foods you are accustomed to eating."

Phelps knocked his empty glass on the bar two times. "Luke!" Phelps entered a period of self-reflection.

"You enjoy eating, don't you?"

After Luke had poured him another, Phelps didn't waste any time securing the glass in his hand. The inner guide watched him raise the glass to his lips. Phelps took a sip of his drink and looked his inner guide square in the eye. "I enjoy drinking more." He winked at him.

His inner guide smiled and nodded. He knew all too well.

"*So, do they*, Danny. You produce an energy for them to consume." His inner guide raised his open hands and spread them. "They've constructed this entire world so that humanity would provide them with this very nourishment."

"What?" Phelps challenged. "You make it sound like we're sheep."

"To the Draco, you are simply that, and nothing more, dumbed-down farm animals for them to control, slaughter and feast upon whenever they see fit."

Phelps scowled. As much as he didn't like it, he knew it to be true. He looked around him at the other people in the bar. He studied Luke, who was now busy polishing glassware, unwilling and unable to expose his patrons even to a news story on television for fear of upsetting them. Then he laid his eyes upon Terra. As much as he truly cared about her, he knew she was oblivious to anything that didn't have to do with seduction and the accumulation of money. She made outrageous money and she didn't spend it on drugs either. She knew what she was doing, but she hadn't a clue what was going on in the greater scheme of things. It was indeed a scheme of diabolical proportions. The bouncer, Phelps mused, when he looked at him mulling about the room, was a complete dullard. 'How would he react if he had come to know the truth about this reality?' he wondered. 'Could he even comprehend it? Could any of them?'

"After they invaded, the Draco Reptilians created your-Society. Then, they introduced your monetary system based upon ancient black-magic debt-slavery; your political system based upon the illusion of choice when the same bloodlines fill the seats of power with their own agents to enact an all-encompassing agenda." He eyed Phelps. Phelps knew he wasn't going to like what came next. His intuition was definitely becoming more and more astute.

"Your legal system is another complete farce as is the criminal justice system and court system." Phelps nodded. He even raised his glass in salutation. No truer words could have been said. "Your educational system is nothing more than indoctrination, and I believe we've already touched on the false religions being shoved down the psyches of frightened, clueless populations of the world's many diverse regions."

"I know what you mean, but say it like you mean it!"

"Humans are slaves! They allow you the false perception that you are completely alone in the universe, while covering up all evidence of past civilizations and off-world intelligences who have visited here for millennia. They make you believe that you dwell on the one blue paradise capable of supporting life, one world among billions, and the rest of the universe is unpopulated and yours for the taking, but as I said, everything you've been taught in school is an outright lie."

"How can *everything* be a lie?"

"It is a monstrous lie inextricably interwoven with the

tiniest bits of truth to keep you confused, confounded, and controlled."

Phelps felt like throwing up.

"Because these institutions are all part of the systemic control grid meant to keep you enslaved in a world whose foundations are chaos and fear."

"I don't feel like the world is built upon fear..."

"Really?" his inner guide interjected. "They have segregated the many regions of this world to keep the people divided and conquered. Long ago, they had introduced pantheons of gods and goddesses for people to adore; to give away their own innate divine power to, to kneel before, to pray to, to worship with their very life essence. Do you know how many wars have been fought between rival faiths, even within the same region? Think of all the people who have not only been marched to their deaths, but slaughtered or sacrificed on the altars of these fake deities. They teach on one hand that the Judeo-Christian God is an all-loving, all-knowing, compassionate God who loves you, yet if you disappoint him for any number of reasons, you'll be cast into the Lake of Fire, to suffer and burn and choke in agony for all eternity. They teach you, out of one side of their mouths, that Christ—the Son of God—can and will forgive all of your sins, but that God is a wrathful, judgmental God who may elect to destroy you at will instead."

Phelps sank on his stool.

"Humans live their lives fearing both God and the Devil. They fear being judged for simply being themselves, when they are truly infinite divine god-lings in the making who can be whomever or whatever they choose to be. They fear death when there is no such thing as death at all. People fear whether or not they'll make it into Heaven or whether they'll burn forever in the flaming pits of Hell."

Phelps grunted. He could find no argument.

"They provide you with the illusion of freedom, the illusion of choice, Democrat or Republican, Pepsi or Coke, McDonalds or Burger King, Christian or Muslim, Right or Left, Gay or Straight, Rich or Poor, Priest or Prostitute, but regardless of the choices you make, or the way you believe things are, or the way you believe you are living your life, you're still firmly in their control from cradle to grave and then all over again through their false light matrix and reincarnation trap."

Phelps became lost in his own inner self-contemplation. Not too long ago, he nearly took his own life when the weight of what he had done came crashing upon him. He took another slug of his drink, swished it around in his mouth, so he could enjoy the sting of the alcohol on his gums. Then, he lowered his head.

"Listen to me," his inner guide continued, lifting Phelps' chin and staring deeply into his eyes. "As long as humanity believes that they're free, they'll never fight for their freedom."

"A lot of people are really tired of fighting the 'system,' as you call it," Phelps said. "The only thing that really happens to people who do is that they get railroaded in the end."

"My point, exactly! It's been designed this way, on purpose."

Phelps set his drink down and moved it away with his extended fingertips.

"This hidden tyranny can go on forever, unchallenged, and it will go on forever—if everyone remains oblivious to the truth."

"So, who are they really?" Phelps interjected. "These Draco or whatever you call them... these Reptilians?"

"They are invaders. They are the Serpent... in the Garden of Eden."

Phelps reached out and retrieved his glass and he slugged

down the rest of his drink. He never before would have entertained a fraction of what he had been exposed to in the recent days, if he hadn't experienced it himself. He also knew that no one else that he was aware of had even the slightest inkling about what was really going on. 'What was his role in all of this?' He wondered. Why was he and seemingly he alone being exposed to this startling, life-changing, reality-bending information?

"Humans were greater beings than you can possibly imagine… once upon a time…"

Phelps winced. "You've got to be shitting me!" It was too much to take. "Look at this world!" He rested his temple in his palm. "Look at the mess we're all in!" He eyed him with suspicion. "Great, how?"

"Perfect physical form," for starters.

Phelps recalled his reflection in the mirror the other day as he went to reach for the shoe and how his physique had so visibly improved, as did his ability to catch the fleeing perp who was so much younger than he was. "What else?" he asked.

"Ageless, intuitive knowing, telepathic abilities…"

Phelps recalled his ability to so easily read the thoughts of the man who was interrogating him in the military base.

"And this is the fun part…" his inner guide mused. "Multidimensional travel…" the words struck home to him "… when he recalled his uncanny ability to move into and out of different realities."

Phelps slapped the bar with his open palm. "That's…" He spun around in his stool as if a light had come on inside his mind. "…what just happened to me in the back woods."

"Indeed."

"You call that fun?" He scowled a bit, although he had to admit, he did find it exciting. "That scared the shit out of me!"

"You are expanding beyond human perception," his inner guide said, confidently. "Beyond the confines of your reality. Within your DNA are light-encoded filaments of energy that contain the total essence of your being, your past, your present, and your future selves, all activated... by light."

Phelps pondered. "So that's what's been happening to me. What about that beautiful woman? I know her! And that place..." Phelps recalled, rapping his fist on the bar. "It was so peaceful, so serene. I just can't even put it into words."

"Welcome to my world Danny. It was your first glimpse of the fifth dimension, and you described it correctly earlier when you surmised it was where we all came from and to where we all shall return. Rather than enjoy a blissful existence in that paradise, Danny, you chose to incarnate here, to take physical form in their false construct—their perfectly-designed mind prison."

"I did?" Phelps guffawed. "Why don't I remember choosing to do that?"

"They manipulated the DNA of the physical forms that would be temporarily taken as vessels through which consciousness could interact here in third-dimension."

"Huh?"

"Why is it that we have been told over and over that humans only use 10 percent of their brains? You've heard that, haven't you?"

"Yes, I've heard something along those lines," Phelps agreed.

"They've shunted your DNA and with so much of it lying dormant or remaining inoperative, they have prevented you from remembering who you truly are and why you came here in the first place."

"I still don't understand." He took a sip of his drink.

"Keeping you locked down in a state of blissful ignorance makes you easy to deceive."

His inner guide paused momentarily anticipating Phelps' reaction to what he was about to learn.

"They've been passing themselves off as God from the very beginning."

"What? Seriously, what the hell does that mean?"

The inner guide persisted. "The greatest deception with which the devil has tricked you, was to convince humanity that he is God."

Phelps choked on his drink. "Wait, what?"

The inner guide delved even deeper as he began to quote a well-known Scripture. "And Satan said... behold humankind, for they will bow down before my feet... they will worship me and love me..."

Phelps looked astonished. It all began to make sense. The world was the way it was because the sleeping masses had accepted the greatest evil as the most intimate friend and savior.

In a white flash of light, Phelps' inner guide was no longer seated beside him, but was behind him, walking gingerly around to his left side. "You've been duped, Danny, fooled again and again. Humanity has been falling for the same tricks for thousands of years, leaving you all to collectively believe that you are nothing more than shameful, worthless sinners."

"Are you telling me that billions of people around the world gather together at worship services to gleefully join hands and praise *a false god*, all the while begging him for salvation he cannot grant?"

His inner guide studied him.

"That *is* what you're telling me, isn't it?"

"The supreme irony here is that they worship a false god who has warned them never to worship a false god." The inner guide took Phelps by the arm, and Phelps felt like he was preparing him for a great task. "Come on, Danny. Look at all the red flags. Does this really look like a world in which a truly infinite, loving God reigns supreme?"

Phelps rolled his lower lip under his teeth.

"This imposter even admits that he is a jealous, *angry* God." The inner guide chuckled to himself. "The True Universal Creator does not require worship. That's not divine awareness. That is of the ego!"

"I've often wondered why there could be so many religions..." Phelps added

"The invaders corralled their human livestock among the specific regions of the world and provided them with false deities to worship and spoon fed them doctrines full of lies. They wove in some half-truths, so as to give the dumbed-down masses the faintest glimmer of hope that they could be true. This afforded the Draco the luxury of orchestrating a series of endless, brutally destructive conflicts whenever and wherever it suited them, conflicts responsible for widespread, rapid death, dismemberment, disease, misery, terror and starvation. Mother Earth has been drowning in spilled blood and the Draco Reptilians have been sucking it up like the parasitic, psychotic vampires that they truly are."

That last bit was stoking the fire in Phelps' furnace.

"Is this really the world you want to live in, Danny?"

"No!" Phelps sneered. "Of course, it isn't! Nobody in their right mind would want any of that."

"Well then, why is it you have everything *you don't want?*"

'The God we've been taught to follow is an impostor?' Phelps thought. 'A parasite?'

"Do you have any idea how much energy they absorb from humanity, day by day, minute by minute, simply by feeding the cast-off, negative emotions of misery, despair, depression, and hopelessness so many people feel?"

Phelps felt sick to his stomach.

"If that weren't bad enough, they then convinced billions

of clueless devotees to dress in their finest clothes and lure them into their varied churches, temples, mosques, and synagogues where they feed off the worship and praise the people so eagerly offer up to them."

"Disgusting."

"These parasites even go so far as to pass around the 'collection plates,' while some misguided fool sings a chorus of how beautiful the blissfully unaware people are as they either willfully offer up their money or do so against their will, out of sheer guilt, hoping to buy their way into Heaven. Regardless of how the money makes it into the plate, the intention and the act itself keeps the charade going on into perpetuity."

"If what you say is true, they are insane, diabolical, sadistic maniacs." Phelps said.

"They are drug addicts, Danny. They're addicted to the plethora of negative emotions humanity emits. You are their drug of choice. Their fix." The inner guide pointed away. "You just saw them in the forest!"

"I've never encountered them in all the years I've been on the force. How can they control nearly 8 billion people without ever being seen?"

"Brilliant, aren't they? When they invaded Earth so long ago, they procreated with human females. These master geneticists created a hybrid race—half human—half reptilian."

Phelps sprang up from his seat. He'd reached his threshold. "I gotta get the fuck outta here!" His inner guide grabbed him firmly by the arm.

"Listen to me!" He eased Phelps back onto the bar stool. "This hybrid race has infiltrated the highest positions of power..."

Phelps held his hand up in the air. "I can't take anymore..." He shook his head. "I don't want to know this."

"This bloodline is very powerful," the inner guide continued. "They control every aspect of the System, from the highest, secretive echelons of government, banking, finance, healthcare, science, education, and media to control the narrative, and as we have discussed, their ultimate control mechanism... religion."

Phelps was about to tap the rim of his glass, but he reconsidered. He could dull his senses no more. Distraught, Phelps looked deep into the eyes or his inner guide.

"They don't breed outside their own bloodlines. Deceptions run very deep, Danny. Even they are not the top of this hierarchy. These beings control your world on behalf of this "God"... who created the image of the Devil... a true reflection of itself... and the image of Hell to keep humanity in a perpetual state of fear."

Phelps looked utterly defeated. "Are you saying..."

His inner guide quickly interrupted him. "The god people have been praying to... is none other than... The Devil!"

"The millions of people praying to "God" have been praying to Satan? This is who everyone has been worshipping?"

His inner guide nodded, sensing Phelps' vulnerability—his entire world collapsing down upon him. He walked slowly around to his other side and stepped in closely to be present and to hold space for him.

Phelps felt a heat growing in his gut, one that could not be denied. It was a thirst for truth he had been seeking to quench all these long years since his brother's murder, and now that he was drawing closer at last, he stood on the precipice. "Everything we've lived... is a lie!"

"Aren't you tired of it," the inner guide queried, encouragingly.

"I am..." Phelps replied, tugging at his hair by the roots. He drew the deepest breath he had ever drawn and when he collected his thoughts, he said, "I am so very tired of it all." Distraught, he hung his head. "I just want it to end, honestly."

The inner guide watched intently. "Are you feeling any different lately?"

Phelps' face wrinkled and contorted. "Oh, hell yes, I feel like I'm going out of my mind!" He shook his head. "I don't know what to think." He cupped his hand behind the back of his neck. He glanced at his inner guide and lowered his voice. "You know, I actually *cried* the other night."

"I know," the inner guide admitted.

Phelps reeled back at first. He was having a hard time adjusting to the fact the telepathic abilities his inner guide had been speaking about, were indeed real. He knew it to be true. He had been experiencing it himself.

"It's okay, Danny. As your mother has told you, tears are healing. The chemicals released through them purge the emotional body and allow the physical body to mend."

"You know I'm the only one who didn't cry at my brother's funeral."

Phelps' inner guide pulled him closer. "A clear emotional body makes the spiritual body stronger, more vibrant. Your emotions have connected you with your spiritual body."

The inner guide stared into Phelps' eyes. He sensed the building acceptance which further encouraged him. "Remember 'Who You Are' and why you're here. Remember the world before they arrived. Remember what happened." He tapped Phelps in the center of the forehead. "Just remember!"

Distressed, Phelps rested his head in the center of his folded arms on the edge of the bar. His inner guide pressed his fingers against Phelps' temple. A light flashed inside and the memories of his first incarnation in human form overcame him, memories experienced as a fully-empowered man named Xandrathu.

* * *

Xandrathu turned abruptly in the tall, swaying grass and

focused his attention skyward. He forced his eyelids shut and centered himself. His pineal gland pulsed and expanded in a flash of violet light. His beautiful companion Solara smiled as she approached him from the distance, her long, black hair swaying in the soft, warm breeze as it caressed the rolling plains and passed eastward. Her translucent white dress hung just a few inches above the top of her bare feet and shimmered in the light of the brilliant, radiant Sun shining overhead. She pursed her lips briefly when she sensed her loving companion's roiled emotions. Solara cupped her delicate hand around the nape of his neck and squeezed tenderly as she leaned in around toward his face to learn what was troubling him so. She studied the subtle movements of his eyeballs behind the thin, pink flesh of his closed eyelids. There they rapidly darted back and forth, from left to right. After his eyebrows furrowed, she decided to reach out with her own innate psychic awareness to identify the nature of his distress. When she saw what it was that he was discerning, their mouths fell open in unison.

Xandrathru opened his eyes and the couple pointed to and gazed toward the sky in horror.

"Invasion!"

Panic permeated the local quantum field and quickly overrode the feelings of peace and tranquility that permeated every aspect of their daily lives.

He knew, instinctively, that a great war had taken place outside Earth's atmosphere and that the dark, victorious, malevolent beings were about to take possession of that which they had no right to obtain. These beings, he knew, would become known in the annals of history as 'Those Who from Heaven to Earth Came,' those who had fallen from above, or the 'Fallen Ones,' or more recently, the 'Fallen Angels.' He also discerned that they were nothing more than interdimensional, extraterrestrial life-force-sucking invaders who intended to claim the world that would become their newest colony among thousands.

Xandrathu gasped as a gargantuan, pulsating, platinum sphere began its slow decent through Earth's magnetosphere, and with it, a turbulent mass of gigantic storms.

As it hovered overhead, thousands of smaller, silvery egg-shaped craft shot out and away from it, sweeping down in one great arc like a flock of metallic birds, twisting and turning until they dove into the atmosphere and streaked down toward the unsuspecting world.

Perpetual clouds of misty rain shrouded the swamps and bogs and creatures both great and small gazed up past the horizon to witness their arrival. The animals withdrew and took shelter inside the many rocky crags, wooden knells and tall grasses.

The invaders had come.

As the landing craft touched down, the natives blinked repeatedly in their direction, sharing uneasy glances, not knowing what to do, if indeed there was anything they could do at all.

The landing ramps descended and out came wispy beings made of a darkness that would stand out completely even in the pitch-black evening hours. As they descended, their bodies shifted and transformed from translucent, shadowy wraiths into hulking bi-pedal beasts with glistening green scales and bright and terrible yellow eyes. They hissed and growled once their large bare feet touched the moist swamp grass. They gurgled and cawed once they dug their other-worldly talons into the muck.

Solara wheeled behind the muscular frame of her beloved soul mate and peeked over his shoulder as he scanned the interior of the great ships with his mind. He sensed some-thing foreign, far away from any emotion he had ever expe-rienced in the 863 years of his current life. Whatever this encounter portended, he vowed to do everything in his power to protect his beloved and his people with every fiber of his being.

The natives had never known violence, so the strange invaders easily rounded them up by the necks and threw them to the ground, as the Winged Overlords stepped off the ships and made their presence known at last.

Xandrathu, like those who did not fall immediately to their knees in subservience, were cut down by blistering beams of light from devices the early humans did not at all understand. The wounded were beaten down and devoured for all of their terrified clansmen to witness. The fairest women were snatched by their hair and dragged off into pens where they would await their turn to be used and abused, however the tyrannical creatures saw fit.

Phelps reached out as if he could interact with the scene slowly fading before his inner eye where the early humans were strapped to metallic operating tables, poked, prodded and experimented upon by the emotionless serpent-like scientists who poured out their disdain, their hatred and malice.

When Phelps could take no more, he nearly fell back off his stool. His inner guide caught him. Phelps rubbed his eyes when he had finished recalling the last moments of his very own past life during the invasion. "I... I was there!"

His inner guide grabbed both of his arms. "Yes!"

Phelps' nostrils flared. "They murdered me... and my people! They stole everything I held dear..." Phelps wept. "They tore the world to pieces, including my beloved soulmate."

"And now you can turn the tide..."

Phelps shook his head. "Your challenge is too great," Phelps replied, flatly. "I can't do this!"

He began to see a bright, glowing radiance of golden light in his lower periphery and when he lowered his chin to look down, he gasped.

The inner guide smiled brightly at him.

The fire Phelps felt growing inside his core was now clearly visible.

"Your true power is now becoming clear!"

Phelps turned to look into the many mirrored faces behind the bar and more than simply astonished, he was equally both jubilant and awestruck. His entire body was *glowing*—brightly—the result of a brilliant shimmering sphere of liquid light expanding from the center of his chest to fully encompass him.

"Your purpose here," his inner guide gently revealed to him, "...Now in this lifetime, is to make a stand!"

Phelps felt this power expand to envelop his body and consume him.

"...Once and for all to rid this planet of the Reptilian presence!"

"I've failed once," he said, looking down at his outstretched arms and palms. "What makes you think I won't fail again?"

Phelps stepped back to behold his inner guide now shimmering inside his own brilliant white aura which was pulsating and contracting in waves.

"You can do this, Danny! You *can* do this!"

The fierce battle between Phelps' fear and courage was raging like a firestorm within. Every memory of his life before this point was flashing before his eyes.

"Unlike the last time, you can now fight them *on their own turf,* Danny! They, like the ones in the forest would never expect it. They won't know what hit them!"

Phelps felt a sudden tingle on the top of his head and his

inner guide grabbed him firmly by the shoulders and locked eyes with him.

"*You* are the *Renegade of Light!*"

In his mind's eye, Phelps saw his younger self once again standing defiantly in his parents' living room, withdrawing the magnificent, shining samurai sword from its sheath and filling the room with the sound of ringing metal.

As the last remarkable images of his vision dwindled like a candle's flame and faded away into nothingness, tears of hope and inspiration welled up in his eyes and spilled over down the sides of his cheeks. He could not deny the inner guide's confidence in him and the hope he now had for all of humanity. Phelps knew that he had finally and most assuredly stepped to the precipice and that only his faith in both himself and in his newfound purpose would give him the strength and resolve to continue.

The inner guide grabbed Phelps by the shoulders and maintained the serious lock on his watering eyes. "Embrace... and fulfill your destiny!"

The image of the man before him erupted into a blinding white light which began slowly transforming before Phelps' astonished eyes into a likeness that was becoming more familiar with each passing second. As Phelps witnessed this, his heart exploded with love and illumination.

Tears streamed down his face because he came to the sudden realization that the enigmatic inner guide was never a stranger at all, but was instead, Phelps' own highest awareness, his fully-empowered and fully-activated multi-dimensional self, who had been watching him since the moment he drew his first breath and reaching out to him from the highest spiritual dimensions and encouraging him to become that which he was meant to become. "I will never leave you..." he said, the voice echoing in his mind.

With tears in his eyes, Phelps fell into his embrace and felt the light of 1,000 suns radiating within him.

"Because, I... AM you."

And so begins the most profound and awe-inspiring transformation the human race had ever conceived... the birth of a new, fully empowered, fully-activated human species.

If you've found this book interesting, the Authors would sincerely appreciate it if you would take the time to write and post honest reviews on amazon.com, barnesandnoble.com, goodreads.com and tell your friends about the book on your favorite social media platforms.

Please visit the official Renegade of Light website for news, merchandise and information on the upcoming releases in the Renegade of Light Series and personal appearances and signing events by Dennis E. Higgins and Jason McLeod:

www.renegadeoflightofficial.com

To watch the original Renegade of Light Movie Trailer, visit:
https://www.youtube.com/watch?v=EINfNLRspTw

Please visit author Jason McLeod's websites for more information his books and personal appearances at paranormal, new age and spirituality conventions:
www.mcleodmetaphysics.com
www.darksiege.com

Dark Siege: A Connecticut Family's Nightmare

You never really know what can be lurking in the cemeteries you casually drive by. Such was the case in the Fall of 1993, when Linda McLaughlin and her innocent six-year-old daughter Kelly passed by Easton Connecticut's Union Cemetery on a stormy afternoon just days before Halloween. Kelly didn't know such spirits existed when an apparition materialized and tapped into her consciousness. Nothing could have prepared her for the suffocating terror that she would soon experience when it followed her home.

The merciless spirit didn't stop with Kelly. It targeted each and every family member and their friends when they were alone and when they were most vulnerable. Then it targeted the alpha of the family, the wealthy, Real Estate Broker father, who was a natural skeptic and the last person to believe in ghosts.

In this terrifying true tale of haunting phenomena, a Connecticut family is plagued by evil spirits who infest their home. Will they ever get their lives back? Will these evil spirits continue to haunt them or will the family find help in ridding them of this terror from beyond the grave?

This book explains in detail the process of investigating a 'haunted house' and what can be done about it. It explains the dangers involved with the negative occult and how dabbling in it can summon darkness and ruin into our lives which could last forever despite our every attempt to stop it.

Jason McLeod is a paranormal investigator, who has spent the last 30 years researching and writing about the activity that plagues people as well as helping individuals and families with the spirits who linger in their lives. He is one of only a few true proteges of the late Ed and Lorraine Warren, the bestselling authors, movie consultants and pioneers of the modern paranormal investigation craze that thrives to this day.

Dark Siege is a 427-page novel written in a cinematic writing style that makes it impossible to put down, but difficult to read at night. What makes Dark Siege totally unique is the 100-page Chapter Analysis Section where McLeod explains the science and spirituality behind the paranormal through Quantum Physics, The Universal Laws of Attraction, Intention and Conscious Manifestation.

NON-FICTION / SELF-HELP
WWW.DARKSIEGE.COM

Don't miss McLeod's Breakout #1 Bestselling
Paranormal Powerhouse

Dark Siege:
A Connecticut Family's Nightmare

www.darksiege.com

Dark Siege 2: The Nightmare Returns

In this true tale of demonic revenge, a Connecticut family, their friends, and their pets face the most vicious and wicked repercussions imaginable for standing up to the demonic spirits who have invaded their world.

In the late evening hours, after a demonic spirit invades her home and penetrates her mind, psychic medium Yvonne Saxon receives a series of horrific visions. These visions reveal the diabolical spirits' plans to exact their revenge on everyone who was in any way involved in the McLaughlin case just two months earlier.

After several unsuccessful attempts to get through to and warn the family and her colleagues, Yvonne makes a last-ditch, desperate call to the Archdiocese in Boston—specifically, to Bishop Marcus Phelan, who had previously been so instrumental in that case.

Bishop Phelan realizes the grave danger they face when he meets misfortune while setting out on the long drive to Connecticut. Will he reach the beleaguered family in time? Can he save his friends from the savage attacks Yvonne has revealed to him in her desperate plea for help?

Dark Siege: The Nightmare Returns is the continuation of McLeod's most terrifying case of diabolical Infestation, Oppression, and Possession. His work was first published in his best-selling debut novel, Dark Siege: A Connecticut Family's Nightmare. Like its predecessor, it is a must-read for any paranormal enthusiast, investigator, or researcher—and most of all, for anyone who had endured, or who is currently experiencing paranormal activity for themselves.

This book is a paranormal powerhouse. What makes it truly unique is McLeod's chapter-by-chapter analysis where he explains spirit activity through Quantum Physics, The Universal Laws of Attraction, Vibration, Intention, and Conscious Manifestation.

NON-FICTION / SELF-HELP

WWW.DARKSIEGE.COM

The Nightmare Didn't End There
Delve into The Terrifying True Tale of
Diabolical Retribution

www.darksiege.com

Our Journey Home: The Handbook for the Transition

Imagine how much more fulfilling it would be, if you could experience an entire lifetime free from even the slightest fear associated with your eventual death. What if you could finally know that though the physical body will surely fail, nothing can affect the eternal, immortal, ever-lasting being that you are in your purest form?

Suppose that reading one book could answer the most mysterious questions about what happens when your body is undergoing the dying process and what happens to your consciousness once you draw your final breath?

You are about to read that book.

In reality, there is no death at all. It is an end to your most recent journey, an exploration into temporary physicality, but it is not the only journey you will take, and it will certainly not be the last.

Death of the physical body is certain.

It is time that you know what awaits you when that happens.

No one in the history of the earth has ever 'died.'
They have simply changed form.

Lose Your Fear of Death and Dying
A Large Print Illustrated Guide to the Afterlife
The Culmination of 30 Years of Paranormal
Investigation

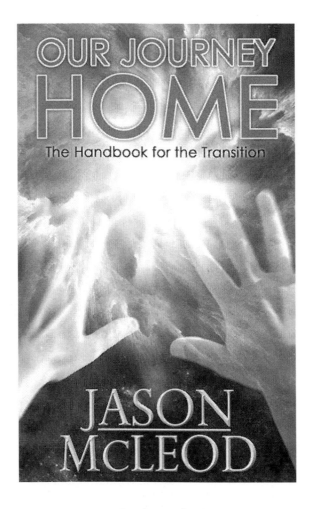

www.mcleodmetaphysics.com

Are YOU a RENEGADE OF LIGHT?

Are you helping make the world a better place by intending, visualizing and creating a world of peace, joy, abundance, prosperity, love, compassion and freedom for all of humanity?

Are you making an effort to awaken others?

Please tell us why YOU are a RENEGADE OF LIGHT. Visit www.renegadeoflightofficial.com and become a vital part of the Renegade of Light Movement by sharing your story with us and the world on the I AM A RENEGADE OF LIGHT BLOG.

The Authors will personally review and select some of the most outstanding posts and award the winners with coupon codes for discounted merchandise, including T-Shirts, Sweatshirts, Hoodies, Beach Towels, Stickers, Posters and more...

Made in the USA
Columbia, SC
10 August 2019